A Rough Road

An Australian Story

Lyn Bodycoat

A catalogue record for this book is available from the National Library of Australia

Linellen Press
265 Boomerang Road
Oldbury, Western Australia

Copyright © 2018 Lyn Bodycoat

Second Edition: 2019

All rights reserved.

ISBN: 1876922532
ISBN-13: 9781876922535

Foreword

This is a ghost memoir based on the life of Florence Brown, my grandmother. In this story the writer adopts the persona of Florence. Fleeing from the clutches of the IRA and the Irish Troubles, Florence and Bill struggle through the Depression and create a life for their family in early times in Western Australia. It covers life in the Goldfields, the farming areas and describes the fear-laden lives of ordinary people living in this era. The loneliness and homesickness of these people cannot be overstated. It starts in 1928 and ends two decades later.

Both Flo and Bill have been given a voice in the book, as it was felt that <u>A Rough Road</u> was the journey they both embarked on in their courageous departure from their home country of Ireland. Incorporating social and political commentary, this memoir describes a context for strugglers, migrants and Aussie battlers. It concludes when Bill comes home from the war, after winning an MBE for the work he did in a POW camp, and this creates another struggle in their rough road.

Both Flo and Bill were born in 1900. Bill died at the age of 59, Flo at the age of 69.

Lyn Bodycoat

CONTENTS

Foreword iii

CONTENTS v

Acknowledgments vii

Chapter One 1

   The Arrival, 1928 1

Chapter Two 7

   Belfast 7

Chapter Three 13

   A Trip to the Goldfields 13

Chapter Four 18

   Mrs Mason Saves the Day 18

Chapter Five 24

   In the Bush 24

Chapter Six 31

   The Arrival of Moreen 31

Chapter Seven 36

   Winter Ends 36

Chapter Eight 42

   A Heavy Heart 42

Chapter Nine 48

   The Depression Begins, 1930 48

Chapter Ten 54

   Christmas is Coming 54

Chapter Eleven	**59**
A New Car	*59*
Chapter Twelve	**65**
The Commonwealth Bank	*65*
Chapter Thirteen	**70**
A Surprise for the Family	*70*
Chapter Fourteen	**76**
Beulah joins the Family	*76*
Chapter Fifteen	**82**
Letters to Audrey	*82*
Chapter Sixteen	**86**
70 Aberdare Road – Shenton Park	*86*
Chapter Seventeen	**91**
The Move to Rivervale	*91*
Chapter Eighteen	**95**
Death of a Child	*95*
Chapter Nineteen	**100**
The War Begins	*100*
Chapter Twenty	**107**
The Ending of the War	*107*
ABOUT THE AUTHOR	**116**

Acknowledgments

Thank you to the Carnamah Historical Society of Western Australia for the use of some of the photographs. Also thank you to all my family who have contributed stories that have now been recorded for generations in the future.

Chapter One

The Arrival, 1928

My hands felt sweaty as I lugged my huge suitcase along the concrete and took a few steps further in the queue to enter this strange country. Even with Bill beside me, I felt uneasy as I heard unfamiliar voices around me speaking their own brand of English. Slowly, but surely, we passed through customs and soon we were standing on the hot footpath in Fremantle – the port for Western Australia – and our new life was about to begin. It was the summer of 1928 so, with baby Kathleen on my hip, my stomach lurched with excitement.

Six months earlier we had decided to leave our home in Ireland. Bill was a British soldier based in Belfast and I was a twenty-seven-year-old impressionable girl living with my family in Finaghy. As soon as I met Bill I had been attracted to him – perhaps it was the uniform – and I know he felt attracted to me too. However, that uniform was to prove difficult for us and was part of our decision to migrate. I had heard stories of good Catholic girls who had been tarred and feathered after 'consorting' with a soldier and I didn't want that to happen to me.

Our wedding was a quiet affair on a beautiful Irish sunny day in July. For the first few months we were blissfully happy leading the carefree life we had expected but soon that was all about to change. I felt unwell, lost my appetite and realised that I was expecting a child. The weather turned quite quickly that year and before long those cold days of the Irish winter set in. Bill's work demanded long hours and I occupied myself knitting booties for our new arrival. I was very excited, though a touch apprehensive, as I had heard that childbirth was painful. Living with my family was fun really, as I enjoyed our dinner time conversations and the companionship of my siblings

One cold evening in April when Bill was at his barracks and I was sitting in front of the fire with Elsie and Renee, I suddenly felt unwell. It was my younger brother, Donald, who first noticed that I had become quiet and he could see that something was wrong.

"Are you all right Flo?" he said quietly in one of the gaps in our conversation.

My labour pains began quite slowly and soon I realised that the child was going to make its way into our world! After two days of excruciating pain Aunty Mary decided to run for the doctor. It had been raining heavily and I was concerned that the doctor may not be able to help me, despite Aunty Mary's reassurances. I gave birth in my tiny bedroom upstairs in the early hours of a freezing cold day. The dreary weather served as an omen. My tiny baby girl didn't make a sound and, at first, I didn't realise that anything was wrong.

We buried baby Florence, our stillborn child, in a little church yard with a full Catholic mass and communion. I felt sad and numb, like the whole last year had been a waste. The weather of course continued to be typical of April weather – continually wet and cold. I don't know what accounted for my sadness and morose that I couldn't shake off. My sisters and Donald did their best to cheer me up and we took regular trips into town to look through the shops, stopping here and there to admire the clothes. Dressing in black only added to my grief when I reflect on that time in my life and soon even Bill became tired of trying to cheer me up as the weeks dragged on.

We stood waiting for the weekly bus to Safety Bay for ages,

patiently standing under a tree, which itself was waiting – waiting for its weekly water. I wasn't accustomed to seeking shade, but I soon realised that this was a way to escape the heat and the glare of the cloudless blue sky. My flimsy sandals struggled with the sand and I longed to sit down. Soon the bus screeched to a halt in front of us and, with the dust swirling to a standstill, I climbed up the steep steps and found a seat while Bill and the driver put our cases in the luggage compartment. The wooden seats made my legs uncomfortable as the sweat made my legs stick to it but soon I was able to settle back and enjoy the bumpy ride over the gravel track to our new home. I felt my eyes wanting to slide down to provide me with some rest, so I let the eyelids gradually fall and listened to the conversations around me. A man behind me was telling a stranger how he had just come from the Maylands Aerodrome and he had heard that the Commonwealth Government was going to spend five thousand pounds on an upgrade to ensure that big planes could land safely in the future. He continued by saying that a big pumping apparatus was going to ensure proper drainage for the aerodrome. At least that's what I think he said; their voices were so strange. It was nice to think that plans were being made for the future and that something productive did happen in this land that seemed so quiet and hot, compared to the metropolis of Belfast. A friend of Bill's had organised the purchase of a very modest house in a remote area of Western Australia, which was as far away from Belfast as could be and here we were!

The bumps and dust continued for some time until I noticed there were a few more houses to be seen. I became alert when I heard Bill cough and felt him move in the seat beside me.

"Are we there yet?"

The smell in the air suddenly became quite different; the smell, which was later to be known as the smell of the sea, had a certain coolness about it. The sound of the engine of the bus changed as I recognised a slowing of our motion. My heart skipped a beat as I thought, "We're soon going to be there at 21 Safety Bay Road in this place called Safety Bay, and a chapter of our new life is going to unfold."

As we turned into Safety Bay road I could see a wooden house with an old tin roof right on the corner. A corner house! Oh, my goodness, I couldn't believe that a house with such a big yard could be mine because, as we drove nearer, I could see a number saying 21 on the letterbox. In my mind I could hear the house begging the bus to stop right outside – and it did.

The driver called out, in his tired voice, "Brown."

"That's us," I whispered to Bill excitedly. I could see Bill stretching his neck so he too could have a good look at the house and its surroundings. I stood up and alighted from the bus and stared at the house. Bill struggled with our suitcases and I realised I needed to help him. Noisily the bus left us, surrounded by its dust, but when it settled I dumped my case and hugged Bill. When we entered through the gate, which was only just hanging on its hinge, we were on a well-worn track leading to the back door. A Lilac tree provided some beautiful shade, but I was interested in the three steps that lead up into the house.

"Quick, Bill. Can you find the key?"

He took this enormous key from his pocket and put it into the keyhole. It turned easily, and we stood on the wooden verandah, splinters and all. I could see the copper in the corner next to the cement wash trough as I walked towards another door. It squeaked when it opened and as I stepped inside I could smell dust and past cooking smells from the family before us. Lots of cupboards, I thought, though I didn't have much to put in them. I walked through the next door into the passage and could see the glass and wooden front door that clearly no-one used. At the end of the little passage were three bedrooms, the largest one ours. All the walls were white-washed, and some parts of the ceiling looked like they were to about to droop. I dumped my suitcase on the wooden floor and flopped on the horsehair mattress on the wire bed. I had come all the way from Belfast and now I was home! Little Kathleen, too, was exhausted!

Some loud screeching woke me up next morning, so I clambered out of bed and made my way to the verandah to see what had disturbed me. There it was again, so I looked up to see if I could work out the sound's direction. Several large white birds flew over the sand hills towards the beach, screeching loudly as they went. What a loud noise from a bird, I thought and soon Bill came to join me. There was so much bright blue sky, and this was so very different from our sky at home, which was always grey and threatening to rain.

I must begin to think that this was home now so, as I went back inside, Bill remained on the verandah with Kathleen. Soon he came into the kitchen carrying some wood so the Metters stove was lit and the kettle filled with water. Thankfully our landlady had left us a few bare essentials, and having a morning cup of tea was one of those essentials.

"I don't have to arrive at the employment office until tomorrow," Bill said as he sipped his tea. Work would consist of a bus ride to Fremantle and then another bus to the Employment Agency in Perth where he would look for work. The day passed with us unpacking our meagre belongings and walking around the house to get used to all this open space, something to which we were very unaccustomed.

The next day arrived soon enough and we walked to the bus stop shortly after dawn, with the hot sun beating down on us. Kathleen slept fitfully in her old pram and I wondered if every day was going to be as hot, but I guess we had arrived in summer, so this is what was to be expected. Before long the orange post could be seen in the distance and we hastened our pace knowing that the end was in sight. We could hear the old motor in the bus long before we could see it but soon Bill was climbing briskly up the steps and waving to me from the back window.

As the bus became a tiny dot in the dust, I began to think about walking back and hoping the little shop on the corner would be open so I could buy some bread and milk. Yes, the shop was just opening its doors. As I entered, a voice from beneath the counter wished me a good morning. A tired, middle-aged woman lifted her head and asked if I had a billy for my milk. Silly me, of course I didn't have a billy for my milk, so she lent me one and wrapped up some dry looking bread in brown paper, which I promptly took hold of, paid for, then off I trudged home. Whilst walking with the pram my mind slowly drifted off to Ireland.

Chapter Two

Belfast

It always seemed to be raining in Belfast and the winter of 1910 was no exception. Darkness seemed to pervade every corner of our tiny house and even Mum seemed to droop every day, despite the open blinds and the feeble sun trying to peep in on the odd occasion. As I trudged out the front door the noise of guns exploded in the next street. The sounds of people running and men calling out roared through the foggy morning air.

"Get inside, girl," shouted Mrs McCleery, but I continued unabated, slinking along the damp wet grass which was cold on my feet. We lived in a mainly Protestant estate, Finaghy, but we were Catholics, so I knew we had to be careful – but of what I wasn't sure.

Dad had come home late last night after his work in the local vegetable warehouse, whispering late into the night and I could hear him talking to Mum. The close proximity of all our rooms ensured we could always hear what was said, despite their whispering.

"They want me to take on some extra work driving a van and doing deliveries into the area beyond the fence. It would earn us an extra few bob a week. If I don't do it, then I think my name will be first on the list to go."

Dad was always frightened of losing his job and his fear was well founded as the shed was owned by the others. Later, I discovered that *others* were Protestants who were the enemy and in the majority in our area. Dad had always told us to keep our heads down and say nothing to anyone who asked. It was all a bit strange but now I had turned ten I was learning things from others around me, as well as the kids at school. I wasn't going to share any information with my siblings.

I can only assume Dad took the extra work as we started to have dinner without him and Mum left his dinner in the oven hoping it would stay warm as the fire died down at night. When the fire went out we all went to bed to stay warm. Our tummies were full and we were thankful for the stale vegetables and left-overs Dad bought home from work. It was a horrible smell that he brought home and he hated his work but "work was work" and he was grateful he could feed his family, unlike others in the neighbourhood.

I continued to listen to their talk after we all went to bed and, because I was the eldest, I seemed to be awake when Mum and Dad retired for the night, so my favourite occupation became listening to snippets of conversation. I knew Dad was doing extra deliveries, but I couldn't understand why this was so subversive. One night Mum asked him if it was fresh produce he was delivering.

"Sort of," said Dad and, with that, I went to sleep. The sounds of snoring through the thin walls meant that my listening was over for the night, so I rubbed my feet against each other to keep warm which enabled me to go to sleep.

Dad's work became later and later and one day he told Mum he would come home for dinner and then go out again. We were happy with that as it meant we would all eat together and watch the fire as we talked about our days, just like we used to. I was glad we took it in turns because my younger sisters, Renee and Elsie, always talked about nonsense. How they could be interested in such mindless things, I didn't know. By the time it was my turn, I had finished the dishes with Mum and had also completed my job of bringing in the water from the outside tank ready for the morning.

Our days continued much the same throughout that winter and I was so pleased when March arrived, and our days became longer. The rain continued of course, but with less intensity, and soon it wouldn't be such a struggle to stay warm. We all hated winter, with all the washing draped near the fire each night and being confined indoors after our busy days. Dad continued to go to work after tea and I continued to be curious about his words to Mum - "sort of." I slowly formulated a plan to investigate what he was doing. I decided to sneak out of the bedroom window after the kids were asleep, while Mum was doing her jobs.

It all happened the following Monday night when I opened the bedroom window just before the little ones went to bed.

"It's hot in here," I said as I opened the window as wide as I could, knowing that despite my slender shape, it would still be a squeeze for me to get through.

"Why are you putting your shoes on?" asked Elsie as I squeezed into my only pair of shoes that were already too small for me.

"I'm just seeing if they fit me," I lied. I knew I was acting suspiciously but they were ready for bed, so I was hoping their tiredness would creep in and then they would leave me alone.

At last my moment arrived. I shut the bedroom door while I could still hear Mum bringing in the coal from our supply just outside our back door for tomorrow's fire. As the door slammed, I used the noise to make my escape into the overgrown garden bed outside the house. I could see Dad's bulky shape as he opened the creaky gate then walked towards the warehouse. It was dark enough and yet light enough too, so I knew I had to stay out of sight. I crept from one coal bin shadow to another until the big shed came into sight. The smell of fresh manure and rotting vegetables filled my nostrils and made me feel nauseous, but I knew I had to control my churning stomach despite its attempts to continually turn over..

The shed was surrounded by large trees so I was confident no-one could see me but that didn't stop my heart from racing in my chest. My hands felt sweaty, but the night was cool and thankfully the cloud cover increased the darkness. If Dad found me here all hell would break loose!

I stood still and hoped my racing heart couldn't be heard. Thankfully, shuffling and banging noises were heard coming from the shed! After what seemed an eternity, I could hear a solitary engine approaching from a distance.

"This must be it," I muttered quietly to myself. I looked out, careful not to be observed as two men alighted from the truck. Their cigarettes lit the area, so I could see their faces, yet they were unknown to me. I couldn't hear what was being said and I expected some bags or something similar to be loaded. But the two men walked off quickly, almost running, in the opposite direction, thankfully.

Dad finished his cigarette, dropped the stub and jumped up into the truck, which was still idling. He drove slowly towards me down the muddy track and I retreated around the tree until he'd gone. I listened, heard it turn a corner, and took my cue from there. I hadn't come all this way just to see him drive off, so I ran as fast as I could to the corner. The tail lights weren't far away so I was able to watch as I crouched down low against the old building. The idling engine was soon turned off and a man appeared from one of the houses. He looked to be in his working clothes with his cap on his head and his eyes on the truck. He was looking around, but I don't know why as the street was deserted.

Later in the summer kids, including me, would play games in this street until it was time for bed but for now it was quite dark. I heard him talking to Dad, but I couldn't work out what they were saying and soon they went inside.

I ran the last little bit so I could hide in the shadow of the truck, knowing it wasn't going to move any time soon. Slowly I stretched out so I could put my arm up under the canvas cover in a bid to feel inside.

Puzzled on feeling only hessian bags and rocks, I waited until my eyes adjusted to the light, or lack thereof, then stepped up onto the side of the truck to see if I could see anything. I needed to get under the cover so I could feel better, so I opened the back end and crept in as quietly as I could. I could feel hessian bags that were full of rocks and then I could see there were many bags. There were jerry cans of kerosene – I could smell its familiar odour and also bags of fertiliser that I knew were used on the fields, and little boxes of nails, along with tools. I was puzzled by the long sticks with rags wrapped along one end as I could not see any connection between all these items, which I learnt later were tools of destruction and death, designed to cause mayhem and chaos.

My heart raced but for a different reason then and my legs felt weak as I sat down in the back of the truck. I don't know how much time past before I heard a front door unlocking so I quickly gathered my wits and realised I would have to escape from the truck and avoid Dad's wrath. What was Dad doing?

Luckily the two men remained quietly talking on the porch while I retreated from the truck and crept quietly into the dark back towards the safety of my corner. In a state of total numbness, I found my way home and remained shocked in our garden bed under my bedroom window. I couldn't stop thinking about the lie Dad was telling Mum and the mystery of these night trips where strange men talked in whispers. I had heard hushed mutterings of safe-houses, but this house Dad visited didn't look or feel very safe to me.

Chapter Three

A Trip to the Goldfields

When Bill arrived home that weekend he was full of excitement and, as I prepared our dinner, I assumed his fevered state was concerned with a new job, but how wrong I was.

"Just think, Flo, of the opportunities that could come our way if we, too, worked in the Goldfields."

"What are you talking about?"

"Actually, I've taken the advice of the Employment Agency. I met this man called Alf who asked us if we would like to go with him as he heads back to Kalgoorlie. He says blokes are finding gold nuggets and are making their fortune. Imagine never having to be poor again! How tempting is that!"

Soon we were on the train to Kalgoorlie with Alf by our side. I was tired as we had woken early to prepare for this journey, which I really wasn't looking forward to, but I didn't want to disappoint Bill by being a dull wife. I had left Kathleen with the shop lady, Mrs Mason, who would babysit in exchange for some work hours. After all, we had only been married a short time and we had come to Western Australia for a better life away from poverty and conflict on many different levels.

The noisy train continued to rattle, and its rocking would have sent me to sleep if I had been more comfortable, but we were squeezed together in a hot compartment with many others. A baby kept crying and its drone was annoying. Looking outside the window the landscape was red and mainly treeless. No wonder there weren't many animals here; the environment was hostile and foreign. Soon I nodded off to sleep and lent on Bill's shoulder as he talked excitedly to his new friend, Alf. They were both smoking, and the smoke wafted across me as I dozed. In a way it was a comfort as it reminded me of the smoke-filled pubs Dad regularly frequented in Ireland.

As the train screeched to a halt I woke with a start and picked up my case ready to see Kalgoorlie. This place rivalled Perth in terms of population, many people having recently migrated here from the Eastern states. According to Alf, many people from the Eastern states were in favour of Federation, which had happened in 1901, but we were aware of a possible referendum on the succession, or otherwise, of Kalgoorlie from the remainder of W.A.

The township of Kalgoorlie was referred to as Auralia, but that name was fading in its significance as the notion of succession became uncertain. The idea soon faded from the local landscape as pure survival assumed a greater prominence. I was surprised to see the number of people alighting from the train and was particularly surprised to see ethnic people on the streets, so perhaps there were many people like us, just wanting a new life away from past political troubles.

However, when we booked into the *Home Away from Home* hotel the young girl who showed us to our room explained that some of their patrons could be noisy and raucous. When we were on our own Bill and I discussed this, and I thought to myself that the fighting we could hear was probably due to alcohol. How right this thought seemed as I was to see quite a few fights between inebriated men during our few days here. We later learnt there was strong resentment towards non-British men on the goldfields and it was alleged that workers from Southern Europe offered bribes for jobs.

Oh no, I thought. This is just what we were trying to escape when we left Ireland.

"Bill let's go back to Safety Bay. It seems much more peaceful than here."

We were due to meet Alf for dinner in the dining room, which offered some respite for me in this foreign world. The prices were high and therefore few people sat at the tables, but there was a lot of noise from the nearby bar. I was so pleased I had left Kathleen with Mrs Mason.

I went to our room while Bill and Alf went to the bar to meet some locals and consider some work. I had expected more prospecting type of work but apparently the Government was in favour of big corporations at the expense of the little man. I drifted off to sleep, with the noise increasing, but I was too tired to care. Thankfully I heard Bill come in and felt him get into bed. He was aware that alcohol was expensive and we didn't have money to spare. In fact, it was one of the things I loved about Bill; he was careful with our money. How young and naive I was.

Soon we were on the train again returning to Perth and leaving Alf behind to make his fortune. Bill sat quietly in his seat next to me and I wasn't sure if he too would have liked to have tried his hand at making his fortune.

"What a place" he said. "That's not for me. Thanks Flo for reminding me what's important. After those mongrels in Belfast I'm not going deal with mongrels again. I'll find some work elsewhere, you'll see."

"Oh well, lucky we have our home in Safety Bay and no-one can take it from us!"

Seeing how people lived in Kalgoorlie had shaken me up slightly and I was once again reminded of the horrors of poverty and desperation. I thought it would be just so different, but the lines of tents and thin looking men and horses screamed poverty in my head. I looked out the window to see mounds of dirt where men had been digging, clearly unsuccessfully. The dust and dirt seemed to emanate into their clothes and even into the train. Men with wheelbarrows and shovels walked along tracks, the wheelbarrows full of essential goods, such as a tent and billy can. Bill explained that the hessian bag swinging from the handles were waterbags for drinking, clearly an essential item in this hot, dry godforsaken country.

"Does it ever rain?" I asked Bill but he didn't know either.

I couldn't remember seeing many women but those I had seen had tired faces, drab clothes and drooping postures. Sometimes there were young children with them, but it was predominantly an area full of men and everything was so strange.

Even the birds were strange and there were so many different kinds out in the bush at Kalgoorlie. I was only accustomed to the white screeching gulls that swooped around near the ocean. I loved the Willy Wagtail with its long tail, and even little wrens seemed at home in the bush. Lucky, they were at home because, here in the Goldfields, I was an alien who didn't know how to survive. I was pleased when Bill suggested we head back to the train station for our trip back to Perth.

We returned to Safety Bay late at night but with a full moon we could see our way into our home and with great joy I landed on the bed.

"Don't light the lamp," I called to Bill and then the last thing I remember was hearing him moving carefully along the floor, feeling the way with his hands along the wall and then collapsing into bed too. It was still hot but I managed to fall asleep knowing I would see Kathleen in the morning. Hopefully she had enjoyed her time with Mrs Mason.

Chapter Four

Mrs Mason Saves the Day

"Put the kettle on please, Jim, can you?" called out Mrs Mason as we walked through the door of her shop on that hot summer morning. We were delighted to see our little Kathleen run towards us pointing here and there with her childlike babble. She really was adorable but I had a sneaking suspicion that another little bubby was on the way and I had kept this quiet because I didn't want Bill to worry. I recognised the feeling of full breasts and the increasing tiredness but I initially put this down to a new environment and the heat. The morning sickness, too, I had been able to blame on the heat but my increasing waistline was becoming obvious, particularly to someone as astute as Mrs Mason, who was about ten years older than me. She'd had two children and then, quite suddenly, her husband had died so she was left to run the shop on her own. Life wasn't easy for her either and her two sons did their best to keep their little family going, mainly by fishing and doing odd jobs in the immediate vicinity.

"So how did you get on with your Kalgoorlie jaunt?" she asked and our silence probably spoke loud and clear. "If we think it's hot here, then I'm told it's like the desert out there. Oh well, it is the desert I suppose but at least we get a nightly breeze here. We are so lucky to live by the sea. It keeps the ice going just that bit longer."

My face must have registered surprise because she then launched into a long monologue about how difficult it was to keep food cold and in her line of business, the wastage had to be minimal. Oh yes, the ice chest was that box in the corner with a small stream of water dribbling from the bottom. I could only assume it was full of food for her to sell.

Just then Ron brought in three mugs of tea and hoped we didn't mind black tea as the milk hadn't arrived yet. It was due at ten o'clock and it was delivered each day by horse and cart. According to Ron, it was lucky Kathleen liked milk as she had ensured that none of it had gone to waste.

"That's what they survive on Ron even though she's started eating like us," I said. I didn't think Ron was very bright but perhaps he just wasn't used to young children. He and his brother received limited education, mainly supplied by Mrs Mason, and as soon as they could read and write very basic items, then that was deemed enough. Survival was more important and so each morning they went fishing off the beach or with some of the boat men who may be launching a dinghy at daybreak.

"Look here," she said, "the goldfield isn't for everyone and there are many dead folks out there who thought they could find their fortune and they just didn't." Mrs Mason, who seemed such a strong person, didn't spare her words. "I'm sure you looked like such babes in the wood." That's what it felt like and it was quite ironic that another little babe was just staying very quiet for the moment!

I think it was very fortunate that we had our tea to sip as I felt very despondent and a hint of homesickness had seeped into my thoughts. I quickly managed to push them aside and concentrated on what Mrs Mason was saying. She told us that Eric, the milkman, would be arriving soon and perhaps we could assist her with this to help pay off some of our babysitting.

"What a great idea," I said, and hopefully this could assist me with my despondency. "Perhaps I could serve some customers while Bill lugs the heavy milk canteens. What do you think about that idea?"

She slurped up the last remnants of her tea, heaved her dress up from her ankles and looked as if she was about to alight from her straining seat.

"Yep, I like that idea. You're in no condition to be lifting any great weight around so Bill here can do some work. Mind you, I'm not putting him on any pay roll. I can't put anyone on a pay roll except for Jim and Ron who only just earn their keep. After Eric's been, it can get quite busy as people come in for their daily milk and bread."

Not surprisingly Bill turned and looked at me with a face that registered either surprise or shock, perhaps it was a mixture of both. As Mrs Mason walked out the back door, I said, "Yes, I think Kathleen is going to have a baby sister or brother. Bill, I'm pregnant. I don't really know for sure but my clothes are too tight." I know this sounded naive but I didn't really know what else to say. As this was my third pregnancy, I suspect I was in denial because it didn't suit us at this point in time. Oh well, it was out now as all was revealed by Mrs Mason!

His silence hung in the air for ages but luckily when he did speak, he was reassuring or as reassuring as he could be in this situation. "Oh well, I guess we'll get by," but both of us knew this was a cliche when there was nothing else to be said.

I felt quite relieved, as if by acknowledging it then it was real. Now there was an imminent urgency that Bill find work and find it quickly. Mrs Mason's noise of activity continued out the back which was a blessing as it gave us both a chance to recover from a fact that I should have shared with Bill some time ago. Now he was as scared as I was, and he repeated, "We'll get by," just before Mrs Mason came back.

He stood up and addressed her in the most sincere, quietest voice I had ever heard Bill use. "This Eric bloke who is coming today, do you think he could help me find work?"

"Well, he'll be here soon. Why don't you ask him? He lives on a farm, but I don't know, there seem to be lots of blokes looking for work these days."

I waited outside with Bill and we both looked hard into the distance as if our looking could instill an image to appear on the horizon. The mirage flicked as we strained to see and at long last I could hear an engine roar. Soon a tiny spec appeared, surrounded by dust coming from an easterly direction along Safety Bay Road. Bill squeezed my hand. All of a sudden, my heart lurched with excitement, but just as suddenly I realised it was the baby moving – something I hadn't acknowledged up until now. Well at least it's alive and kicking I suppose. I looked down at my tummy and realised I was getting rather round. At this stage I wasn't prepared to do the maths and work out when the baby was due. Just knowing it was there had been shock enough for one day!

As I was daydreaming Bill had started walking towards the man and the wagon.

"Hello there. My name is Bill and I'm working for Mrs Mason. My job is to give you a hand with those milk kegs." The dust swirled up and Bill's words were lost in the motion of horse and cart. Even I stepped back as the horse seemed so big and in control, snorting and swinging its head this way and that. I guess it, too, was thirsty and tired; goodness knows where it had come from, but I figured its journey had been a long one. Man, beast and wagon moved around to the back of the building and quite clearly it was familiar with the premises. The man, Eric, still hadn't said a word as he leapt from his seat on the cart so Bill repeated his words. "Orright, mate, give us a hand with this one." And so Bill's work started.

Of course, that was my cue to get into the shop with Kathleen and wait for customers. Kathleen played around my feet and I gave her a few shop items to play with – a tin of this and a tin of that – it was quite easy to keep her happy. I put my hands on the counter to look important and then started to think about correct change for customers.

"There's the account book that you need to use when people come in. If you don't know them, then don't give them any credit."

Outside I could hear men's voices in conversation so that had to be a good sign. Anything would be better than the desperation I was currently experiencing, and I could feel the tears swelling up in my eyes. I quickly thought of something else to make that feeling go away and I picked up Kathleen for comfort. This isn't how it should be! I should provide comfort for her and not the other way around. I stood up straight and took stock of myself just before someone came in. I didn't want the capable Mrs Mason to know how vulnerable I felt so I was extra cheerful for the lady who wanted some bread and a few groceries. She had a few kids around her so that somehow cheered me up!

"I'm going with Eric to find some work, Flo" Bill called out as he came running through the door, his back covered in flies. I tried to be cheerful as we all knew this is how it would have to go – this is even what we wanted! It had all happened so quickly. "I'll just go home and throw a few things in a bag. You watch, I'll be home soon with a few pound notes in my top pocket."

He pecked Kathleen on the top of her head and gave me a big hug. I was glad he was excited as I felt totally abandoned – just as I had when my mum had died, leaving me in charge of a household. But I didn't want to think of that.

Half an hour later Bill and Eric had unloaded the milk and Mrs Mason assumed front of house in the shop. Thankfully, she took charge of Kathleen too. There was no-one around except for me when Bill and Eric left in the wagon and headed back into the direction from which Eric had come. The noise of the wheels was loud which was lucky because I finally had the privacy to sob and let the tears run down the dust on my face. I couldn't even wave.

Chapter Five

In the Bush

Bill and Eric arrived in Pinjarra close on dark and by the time they reached the farm house, just a few miles out of town, both men were hungry and tired. For Eric, this was a daily trip but for Bill it was the endurance of the bumpy track over such a long distance. His future was so uncertain, but he was excited about his new adventure in this strange land, though the flies and the dense bush had not featured so prominently in his imagination. The track had been full of potholes because of recent rain and several times they had to stop and hack away to clear foliage and debris out of the way.

"Enid will have some dinner ready, Bill. She always cooks too much and we have other farm workers to feed as well. Come this way."

The smell of meat cooking was heaven and, as others were washing their hands in the wash house, Bill quickly did the same. The communal towel was damp and smelly but the meat was all Bill could think about.

After dinner it was time to discuss business, so Bill and Eric sat on the veranda enjoying a quiet cigarette and listening to the night noises of crickets and cicadas. "I've got an idea for you, Bill. As you can see we've actually got a full house here but my brother who lives at Williams is often looking for more mature blokes like you. He's had a gut full of young fellas who take off after a few nights. I think the isolation gets to them but hey, I think you've got what it takes to rough it on a farm. Also, with a missus and young kid in tow, I figure that some good steady work is all you care about. He'll expect you to work hard and he'll pay you about thirty shillings a week plus keep. How does that sound?"

Bill thought that was the best job offer he'd ever had and was keen to leave for Williams as soon as possible.

"Well, I've got a few more days with the milk run to Rockingham but we could go to Williams on the weekend. That'll be good for Enid too. She likes my brother's wife and they get on well together, so we'll plan on that eh?"

Bill was quick to move to the hut where the working men slept and the kerosene lamp in the distance created just enough light for him to see where he was going as he walked along the stony path away from the main house. Someone must have put the lamp out because before long Bill was awoken by the noises of men washing and moving around and he could only assume it was morning.

His job was to ride around the boundary fence, with an axe and a shovel, to ensure that all the fencing remained intact. That would take a whole day as debris had to be dealt with to ensure fences were secure and the sheep and cows could not wander out into the bush.

Bill thought that this would be quite easy, but he underestimated the ferocity of the bush. It was hard to ride through and Eric's map of the farm was not very clear, but he knew he couldn't ask any questions or get in the way.

However, he first had to help with the milking by rounding up the cows and enticing them into the milking shed. He'd never worked on a farm before but he knew he had to act tough and he watched the others and talked like them too. It was surprising how smoothly the operation went; the cows knew the routine and, of course, they liked the hay that was fed to them during the milking.

The three men and Bill just walked behind the animals, along the fence line, into a smaller paddock and then into the milking shed. Even the dog knew when to stay back, when to bark and when to go close to make them walk through the open gate. Eric met the cows in the shed and his quiet manner and watchful eye ensured that each cow moved into its bale. As this happened the cows began munching on their hay and were oblivious to the noises of shut gates behind them and the clanging of milk buckets moving into position. Clearly, with three cows and three men, Bill was left as an on-looker.

"Just watch how they do it and then have a go with Daisy here. She's the quietest but if you work out how to do this then you'll get on well. Just cup the teat and increase the pressure in your fingers from the top to the bottom." Eric then moved away and left Bill to practise on Daisy under Dennis's watchful eye. Dennis was probably the eldest of the three men.

It smelt like a farm yard with manure in all the men's nostrils but Bill was contented.

The days crept on, with Bill riding his horse each day around the property checking the fences. Apart from moving debris off them he wasn't quite sure exactly what he was checking for so, between this uncertainty and the pain in his body from riding, he quickly forgot about Flo and Kathleen. The pinching of the inside of his thighs from the stirrups and his sore bottom from bouncing in the saddle made for quite an uncomfortable day but Enid had made a lunch for him and he had dinner and a comfortable, if not hard, mattress to sleep on each night, so he was happy enough.

Saturday arrived quickly and this was the day for his move to, hopefully, a more permanent arrangement with some pounds attached as well. He had written a letter to Flo, which he hoped Eric would deliver through his milk rounds with Mrs Mason. The promise of some money in the near future gave him hope and, despite the separation, he felt strong and invincible. He knew this would cheer Flo up too and with a new baby on the way he had to work as hard as he could.

The property at Williams was quite different from Eric's farm and the remoteness was reflected in the bough shed for a home. However, the water tank and windmill were close by and the shade from the trees was a relief from the heat. Bill's trip to the Goldfields had shown him the importance of shade and water and, here in the southern farming land of Western Australia, it was no different. He felt a shiver come over him but he quickly threw it off and reminded himself that he was here for the money and the adventure. He'd been a soldier in a past life so he wasn't going to be put off by the bush. Apparently, there weren't any wild animals or predators so what did he have to be afraid of? Like the horses, Bill was relieved when they finally made it to Smith Brothers farm.

Eric and George were brothers who had come to this part of the world to make their fortune, escape poverty and the relentless of English winters with minimal job prospects. Like Bill and Flo, Eric and George were immigrants who had been promised government land with a government grant. However, it was easy to see why this supposedly attractive offer by governments wasn't very appealing. According to Eric, the two brothers met up about once a month to exchange commodities and to ensure the women had some social interaction.

George's wife, Audrey, was a real trooper! She'd learnt to fire a rifle, and shooting birds to feed the dogs was common practice each afternoon. The dingoes, too, were frightened by gunshots so this ensured the sheep were relatively safe at night. Bill had landed himself in rural Australia and, if he thought an adventure was just for him, he was soon to find out that he was correct. Like Eric's farm, the chickens provided a good food source and vegetables were grown with the help of manure but in this case, it was more about sheep manure than cow manure. An attempt had been made to grow fruit trees and the Mediterranean climate ensured the success of the orange trees and the failure of the apple trees.

Clearly the women enjoyed each other's company and the chatting started as soon as the horses came to a halt. As the wagon was unloaded some men appeared and started taking the horse equipment off the wagon to release the horses, which were then lead away. George and Eric engaged in some backslapping and moved towards the house with the women.

The tents nearby were to house the employees and a man called Tom appeared and shook hands with Bill.

"Welcome, mate. I'm Tom and you'll soon get to know these others. Here is your tent, Bill and I've put your mattress inside. You can load your belongings in here as I assume you're going to stay with us."

The shade created long shadows and the domestic dogs sniffed around Bill's ankles as he carried his knapsack from the wagon to the tent.

"Dinner will be on soon, mate, and then we sit around the campfire and watch the flames shooting their sparks up into the sky."

Bill thought of Flo and realised this was a far cry from Belfast but luckily, she wouldn't be here. She would remain in Safety Bay. It was well-named, he thought, though there was no need to be afraid here. It was probably the loneliness that permeated into the soul as another lot of darkness enveloped him, but he and Flo were beyond that as mere survival was the new norm. As Bill went to bed that night he had so many ideas in his head for his next letter to Flo that it was the first time in his life he had ever been excited about writing a letter.

Chapter Six

The Arrival of Moreen

I grew to like working alongside Mrs Mason with young Kathleen crawling around behind the counter and out into the store room but, as she began walking, I needed to be mindful of the hidden dangers lurking around every corner for a toddler to explore. My other little one kept moving in my tummy and I wondered how I would manage with a new baby to nurture.

Every day the wagon of goods would arrive from somewhere and along with that was the occasional letter from Bill when the milk arrived. He clearly enjoyed working in the bush, but in my last letter I had asked him to take some time off for the arrival of the new baby.

Bill's arrival home was just in time as I had been feeling very much 'with child' and that night I went into labour, with the pains becoming more regular. With the smell of ether in the air and noises of people talking loudly, our little baby girl arrived on the 21st April in 1928 amidst much excitement in the hustle and bustle of the Avro Hospital.

Yes, Moreen Presley had made her presence felt and we were delighted. Bill left soon after to register the baby's name and date of birth at the local post office and do the appropriate paper work whilst it was my role to rest. Honestly, you'd thought I was a queen or a princess with all the fuss they made of me, but still, it was nice to be pampered occasionally and I really didn't want it to stop anytime soon! With those feelings, it was with some irritation when I saw Bill again and I read through the paperwork – he had registered the baby on the current day, the 23rd of April, instead of the day she had been born, and he'd spelt her name wrong!

Really, how could anyone spell Presley as Priestly? I didn't want to tarnish the short length of time we had together and I had been able to smell alcohol on his clothes, which was an entirely new experience, which I assumed he had embraced as part of men's business on farms. I had to suppress my feelings of irritation and save my strength for my homecoming with a new baby and a toddler to manage.

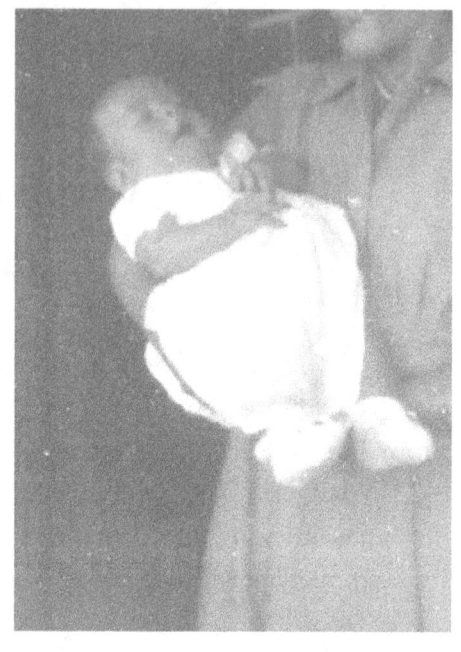

When I waved good-bye to Bill it was quite different this time; so long as he gave me money to manage the household, I realised that somehow, I had gained a new kind of strength and tears were a bit of a luxury that I couldn't quite afford. I had many pensive moments when a surge of homesickness started to creep around me but realised that with no mother of my own, I had no-one really to share my thoughts with anyway. With the smell of the ocean, the noise of the seagulls, and the warmth of the autumn sun, I was happy enough with my life in the care of Mrs Mason. As long as people needed food to eat and stores to survive, the shop would continue to prosper, but soon I was to realise that not all things stay the same. With two small children, I was not as employable as I used to be, but Mrs Mason came up with a plan, which turned out to be my saving grace.

"You're a good cook," she said. "More and more men are walking by and seeking work, so why don't you make them something they can eat whilst they are going by?"

There certainly did seem to be more men just walking by, and I hadn't realised that they were looking for work. This was the overflow from the city and the goldfields. A cold shiver overcame me and suddenly I was grateful for Bill's work in Williams and, even though it was a hardship for him, he liked the company of the men and the feeling that he was working toward a final goal, even though he didn't know what it was! For me, it was the security of a pay cheque in times when others were unfortunately struggling. So, I toyed with the idea of making something but at the same time I had to feed Moreen and amuse Kathleen.

Cooking pies was something that wouldn't cost me a lot of money and, with winter on our doorsteps, I needed to keep the fire burning for warmth so why not cook something and sell it? This was how it all began! I set up a box as a counter between the shop and our house and started to sell pies! The smell of food was a successful magnet for hungry men looking for work and even the locals were enticed by the smell emanating from the counter on the roadside next to the shop. Mrs Mason's boys trapped rabbits and sold them to me so it was a bonus for us all. They would spend hours checking their traps in the bush after their daily sales of fish from local fishermen. We all worked hard and then I would need to feed a hungry baby from time to time as her tiny noise drifted from my laundry basket near my feet. Kathleen loved the activity and strangers would talk to her and so she developed into quite a social child who loved to talk and sing.

Mrs Mason's boys also loved to sing but it was quite different from Kathleen's little murmurs. Loud yodelling, male singing and the occasional shouts were heard each afternoon as the boys went to check their rabbit traps. One day the shouting sounded serious, so I headed off in that direction to see if all was well, as it certainly seemed like there was some sort of drama. The boys had seen a snake that had escaped under some thick bush and were keen to kill it.

"It would make great eating, Flo."

But I wasn't convinced. I had heard about snakes in the bush and how their bite could kill a person. "Leave it alone," I shouted to them, keeping my distance, and then I retreated back to my post near the shop with Kathleen wandering around and little Moreen in the washing basket looking up and smiling at whoever looked her way. I wasn't surprised when they sold me their rabbits, that snake, too, had been offered as a delicacy to buy.

"Why don't I buy it from you, cook it up and then bring some over so we can all share it together?"

Jim and Ron thought this was a great idea and took off quickly with the proceeds of their day at work. Later that evening when I arrived with our stewed snake I had to concede that it did smell delicious and when I tasted it all my taste buds were delighted, even if it was against their better judgement! As we all shared a laugh I realised it wasn't something I did as readily as I used to. Oh well, I'd just have to lighten up a bit, I thought as I strolled back home with my washing basket and toddler in tow. It was a clear sky, late in autumn and the sea air had started to cool quite quickly now. I skipped along feeling good about my snake meal, my laugh and the contentment of my babies. The sound of the waves, which originally sound strange, now comforted me and the smell, too, made me feel at home.

My comfort, however, was to be short lived as the next day, whilst walking across the track to the shop, I saw a snake slither just ahead of us, just a short distance from Kathleen as she skipped along the sand. My scream frightened the children, but I couldn't help it and at once Mrs Mason ran out of the shop towards me.

"What's wrong?" she shouted but I just froze. Little Moreen in the washing basket started to cry. Soon I began crying too as Mrs Mason swept up Kathleen into her robust arms.

"You mustn't cry in front of the children," she muttered but that made it worse and suddenly I just couldn't contain it at all. I think I had let my guard down and then quickly I realised the appearance of a deadly creature had filled me with horror. Why had we come to this country, just because Bill was in the army?

The whole scene suddenly seemed foreign and I was like a stranger in a sparse empty land. Then the southerly wind whipped up, just like the snake could have done.

"Now, now," said Mrs Mason as she hugged me close to her robust bosom and soon I gained control of myself. The leaves of the bush started to rustle, and the sound soothed me. She straightened up and smiled down at me, just like a mother would have done. The thought reminded me that I, too, was a mother so I had to assume some kind of brave persona to reassure the precious little souls who were in my care. We all staggered like wounded animals into the shop to regain composure to deal with the day ahead.

Chapter Seven

Winter Ends

With the bleakness of winter behind us, the days grew longer, and the seagulls' screeches grew louder. I enjoyed their cacophony and the sound of the waves crashing onto the beach. Soon my little family could wander along the sand with the wind blowing in their hair. Yes, this was my home now and, in a reverie, under the warmth of the sun, with Kathleen and Moreen, playing in the sand I let my mind ponder on my own early life as a child in Ireland.

It was always cold and wet, with little warmth in the spring air, and the fire in the house always burning – not too much, as money was short with our large Catholic family in the Protestant area of Finaghy. We hadn't always lived in Ireland, but I cannot remember much about our time in Scotland, in my birthplace of Elgin. We came to live in Ireland when I was a wee one and the reason was, as it always is, better work opportunities. I was pleased that Dad worked in the vegetable warehouse as our food supply was plentiful, unlike other families around us who were not so well off. I remember as a child hearing the crying of hungry babies and seeing thin little faces of my friends. My time for child-like pursuits was limited really, as I was the eldest and Mum was often sick.

When she died I simply kept looking after Rene, Elsie and Don. In hindsight now, I don't even know her cause of death, but she was always coughing and then one day, she simply wasn't there when I came home from school.

At the funeral Dad's face was warped by grief and afterwards his words were "Thank you, thank you." Someone spoke to me and murmured something that I didn't hear. Death had enveloped her and I was scared that it would take me too. I wanted Mum to take my hand, but that hand was in the coffin now. All I remember is that my workload increased as Dad seemed to be away a lot, either at work or in the pub. No-one ever asked why men went to the pub when money was so scare, and no-one ever asked me if I missed my mother.

I was aroused from my daydreaming by the squeal of a child and then I realised I had to be a good mother to my children. I quickly gathered them up into my arms for a big hug and we walked back through the low-level scrub of Safety Bay, across the dirt track and into our modest house, ready to face the day and all that it might bring.

With Christmas not far away, business for Mrs Mason increased and I was stacking shelves as customers came and went. We became friends with our regulars, but I noticed that more of them were slower to pay their bills. We were aware that the economy was slow, but with two children now, it was easier to work in the store than to make pies for road-side sale.

"People will always have to eat and wear clothes," said Mrs Mason when we talked about accounts that were running up more debt each day.

I was anxious that I could be without work, so some ideas began to formulate in my head. "Why don't I see if Audrey and George need me on the farm?"

I mentioned this one day while we were flicking pieces of paper on the counter, as now, part of my job had become accounts management. It seemed that everyone had a role to play, even if it was cutting each other's hair.

Soon I was established on the farm with Bill and we were a family unit again. I had leased out our Safety Bay house to three fishermen who needed somewhere to stay and off I went to Williams! Quite a few men had left the farm, so I took over the role of book-keeper, helping Audrey and being a wife and mother. Soon I found out that men who left had been asked to leave as work was 'rationalised'. I quickly realised the generosity of Audrey and George, as they wanted our family to remain on the farm with the hard-working Bill being happy and contented. I was part of that equation, so I had to pull my weight too.

Despite the isolation, I was happy and, when the newspaper

arrived each month, I read it from cover to cover so I could write to my family in Finaghy. During 1929 a federal election was held and the Australian Labor Party was lead to victory over the incumbent government. My family would be pleased to hear about this as we believed the working man struggled and needed as much support as possible. However, little did we know that the next decade would turn out to be extremely difficult for the working man as the Depression became worldwide.

My Irish family seemed so remote as I wrote my letters but I loved receiving letters, so I knew they would love receiving mine. I could imagine the grey wet days in Ireland with the postman riding his bike down the street delivering his mail with gloved hands to keep out the cold.

Meanwhile on the farm, the weather seemed to be always hot and we quickly assumed the habit of looking for shade. Ironically Bill's main job was to cut down trees and clear land. The government had issued instructions on the methods for forest clearing and each settler was given an axe and a crosscut saw. However, the dilemma of disposing of trees was a problem and burning of both felled trees and standing trees regularly took place. Barbed wire, which had been invented in America in 1873, was provided for fencing but fence posts had to be prepared so it was difficult for new workers to learn these skills. I could see why Bill was very employable and his physical strength was a real asset too. However, I was terrified of bush fires which were a constant threat during summers and men had to use wet sugar bags and green bushes to beat out flames. When these bush fires did occur, the burnt paddocks meant the cows would go hungry. The loss of pasture also meant the milk and cream cheque was seriously compromised and so too were our lives. I was quickly learning about the perils of farming life!

But I was here for twelve months, or at least that was the length of time our little home in civilisation was leased out, so I was determined to learn what I could and make myself useful.

Audrey milked cows and drove vehicles so my job in the kitchen was to cook meals for working men and children. The bustle in the kitchen suited me as my cooking skills had been fine-tuned out of necessity whilst working with Mrs Mason. The wood fire made the kitchen hot in summer but in winter it puffed out its warmth for us all. Kathleen and Moreen were adored by all who saw them, and they quickly developed social skills and made us all laugh. Later, in the afternoon, I took care of the accounts as the children slept, while Audrey baked and tended the garden. An afternoon nap suited us all as we were in the habit of early rising, particularly in summer when the days were long and hot.

Our special entertainment happened once a month when the silent movies were shown, and we would all climb on the truck and go into town. The town hall was where everyone would gather and socialise.

An entry fee of two shillings for adults and sixpence for children was charged. Kathleen and Moreen sat on the floor with other children who all knowingly kept quiet and watched the screen. A pianist was essential for the silent movies to be brought to life and occasionally the wrong piece of music would turn a drama into a comedy. At interval soft drinks and candy were served. We were all reluctant to return home at the end of the night, knowing we would have to wait another month before we would all meet up again. The wet and windy nights, with treacherous gravel or mud, were another endurance before we could be safely tucked up into our snugly beds.

Chapter Eight

A Heavy Heart

With a heavy heart, we returned to our Safety Bay home soon after Moreen started walking. Talk of a gold find at Margaret River, combined with George's decision to leave the farm, had devastated us both. All of a sudden bird noises that had once lifted my spirits now sounded like they mocked us, and the sound of the beach seemed loud and angry. Winter was approaching so the darkness started to close in on us even earlier than expected.

Rumour had it that gold had been found in some creeks near Margaret River, but it was yet to confirmed. It was later reported that the gold was real but by this stage many farmers had left their farms, despite the government assistance. Several years later, in

1933, the impact of the Depression was becoming totally manifested within the south west region and the government of the day stopped a gold rush in its bid to look after British money for farming. Stopping a gold rush at the time was totally tied to the economic circumstances of the day. The premier, James Mitchell, was keen to see the Kalgoorlie area remain the only goldfield, despite its lack of water and the deprivation of its inhabitant. Western Australia was in a state of turmoil and I couldn't help thinking – so much for a Labor federal government. Many people thought this and plans for a succession from the eastern part of Australia nearly succeeded, but that's another story.

My concern was that Bill was out of work. It was a particularly cold winter and I was pregnant. Thank goodness for Mrs Mason again!

"Times are really hard," said Mrs Mason. "I can only share the work with you both so, Florence, you and Bill can decide how you want to earn one weekly wage."

This was acceptable for me with my approaching child making its presence felt daily in my ever-growing tummy. Around the dinner table it was decided that Bill could do all the unpacking of the stores and each night I would show him how to do the book work and accounts. I wasn't quite sure that I could make pies, due to my nausea, so I decided to take in laundry and wash it with my own clothes and try to make some money that way.

The months crept on with little Kathleen and Moreen playing in the bush outside near the rainwater tank and I washed clothes using the scrubbing board and clothes line Bill had constructed out of wire and a large fence post from the farm. Audrey wrote to me and we kept in touch as the regular supply truck continued to visit Mrs Mason's shop. Audrey was unsure whether their decision to leave the farm had been wise as the gold in Margaret River seemed to be as elusive as their dream of becoming rich. However, there were many others at Margaret River camping in tents, much the same as in the Goldfields, just waiting for the magic nugget to be found. Audrey enjoyed the companionship of others and I could understand how loneliness was her constant companion. I felt the loneliness eating away inside me too and I was worried about Bill and his lack of work.

Each night after the children were put to bed, we had a session in which Bill learnt the skills of book-keeping. He didn't particularly like it but was very aware of the importance of learning any new skill to make himself employable. I was mindful that, with small children, my dependence was becoming more entrenched, so this pregnancy didn't hold a lot of joy for me. I was becoming more homesick, for what I wasn't quite sure, as the reality was that Belfast would be cold and people would be unemployed.

My letters from Belfast described a despondency that was not cheerful and despite a decline in shootings and street fighting, poverty was becoming the norm. Elsie and Renee had married and were starting to have children. Little Donald was working in the warehouse with Dad so at least they were all saved from the hunger demon. We, too, had no fear of the hunger demon, as left-overs from the shop formed part of our evening meal and Mrs Mason regularly joined us. Sometimes Jim and Ron, Mrs Mason's boys, joined us but they were quickly growing up now, so they liked to have dinner on their own. How quickly young boys become big boys and, as teenagers, they regularly had work on building sites in the area. By this time the townsite was slowly growing and many more houses were being constructed along Safety Bay Road and Penguin Road. With the increase in commerce it meant that bush land was cleared, and the boys had to go further afield to trap their rabbits. However, they continued to barter with the fishermen, so our meals were largely assured. The boys even showed Bill how to lay the traps and check them each morning as the rabbits were largely nocturnal.

Bill would have preferred the outdoor life, as opposed to doing the Mason accounts, but as my dad would say "work is work" and no-one in the Mason family liked writing so this was work that easily fell our way. As Mrs Mason's debts increased Bill quickly became debt collector as he reminded those who came into the shop about how much each person owed. Bartering was often used and our fruit and vege man gave us potatoes, onions, apples and cabbages in exchange for clean clothes for his family. His wife was ill and, with three children to look after, he was happy to use our laundry services. I'm sure that his vegetables were 'seconds' but we were happy to accept them. Services and produce were swapped, and Bill was the arbitrator – a role he enjoyed! Standing in the shop was also a way to keep the beastly easterly away as the wind whirled around the side of the building and the winter of 1930 seemed to continue forever. He liked to see the supply trucks so that he could help unload and get warm.

The supply trucks were also a way of receiving letters and each day I found myself listening for the drone of the engine in the distance. As I looked out the window I could see dust coming from the tracks as they travelled from either Fremantle or from the eastern end of Safety Bay Road. We gradually grew to know all the people in the neighbourhood as children played in spare blocks and on the dusty footpaths where the occasional person walked. In the afternoons I regularly sat on the front verandah where I could watch the children play. Often other children took Kathleen and Moreen to play in their games and the little girls grew to rely on their company. Their laughter and calling out was companionship for me as I waited knowingly aware that the month of November would bring another little one into the world.

I was pleased when my baby was born in the spring, or at least the beginning of the warm season. The long winter had meant chilblains on toes as we lay in bed at night trying to keep warm and I'm sure that Kathleen and Moreen must have had been cold too. Lucky, they were good babies and they were easily contented. I also think the winter of 1930 was the time I was homesick the most and Bill's continual talk of the old country as home did nothing to abate the empty feeling that, for so many years, I had tried hard to control.

We hadn't decided on a name for our daughter and when Bill came to take me home, and we deliberated where home was, I suggested that we call our daughter Heather, as Bill regularly described the beauty of the purple heather that had grown so abundantly around his parent's house.

"What a great idea," he said. "This will be my favourite child."

I wasn't quite sure this was what I wanted to hear but, as a good wife, I had learnt when to say nothing. I wasn't cross with him, just rather ambivalent really, as I prepared to leave the hospital in Subiaco and travel on the weekly bus to Safety Bay, eager to show Kathleen and Moreen their little sister. Once again, they were in the care of Mrs Mason. What a wonderful person she was!

As we walked up the back steps of the house, little Kathleen and Moreen ran to meet us and to my absolute delight I could smell baked rabbit coming from our kitchen. I knew she would have roast vegetables to accompany our meat and the little girls could hardly contain themselves with excitement. My mood shifted dramatically, and the tiredness suddenly dissipated as I leant down into my children's embrace. The smell of fresh soap in their hair put a smile on my face as I looked up into the doorway of our little house. This was our home and now Heather had come to join us.

Chapter Nine

The Depression Begins, 1930

"Bill, it's nearly Christmas time and I think we should celebrate as we have three little ones. What do you think about that?"

"Nahhhhh. We came here to escape all that religious stuff."

My thoughts returned to our time in the beginning of our marriage when we were still living at home and Dad had warned us about the local hostility towards marrying outside our religions. "They'll get hold of you two with tar and feather - and, Flo my girl, you will suffer the most! Why didn't you just marry a nice local chap, a nice Catholic lad? Plenty of them around and not all of them are out of work."

Dad always went on and on like this and I know if Mum had been alive, she would have agreed with him. If I had done this, I would have repeated the life of my parents and I didn't want that. Bill, dressed in a uniform, looked exciting but as a British Protestant soldier he was on 'the out of bounds' list for any Irish Catholic.

"Oh Dad I know you are right," I begrudgingly replied. "Okay. So, what do you want me to do? Migrate?" And so the idea simmered and gradually the whole process grew legs and gathered momentum. The race took off.

Quickly my mind came back to the present as Bill coughed and Heather cried for her milk. "Why don't we wait until next Christmas and perhaps by then I'll have a real job and a bit more money?"

I didn't say anything, but felt sad that three little girls would not celebrate Christmas that year.

"Why the gloomy face?" asked Mrs Mason. "I can read you like a book."

So I told her about our conversation concerning Christmas.

"Are you seriously concerned for the children or are you feeling sorry for yourself? The children don't know anything about it so why not just let it drop? Perhaps we can order a ham from George when he comes. What do you think about that?"

I hugged her again. She always came up with a solution! With her big arms and buxom chest, she was my second mum. Regularly these arms would wrap around me when I needed a big hug.

I began my pie preparation for the day and kept my thoughts on what I needed in order to survive. The road from Safety Bay to Mandurah was progressing well but with that progress the further out I had to travel with my goodies and three little ones. The smell of meat cooking in pastry wafted through the house as the oven churned out today's saviours. Thank goodness for that road and the hungry men who worked on it. Two dozen pies sounded about right and by then it was time to come home and feed my own family. The heat of the day was still a factor to consider and the bright Australian sky was still something I found hard to tolerate. Today the east wind blew strongly so I knew it was going to be hot.

I took baby Heather, in the old pram, to Mrs Mason who had kindly offered to feed her and settle her while I was on the road with Kathleen and Moreen. "That's it. Leave her here, Love. She'll be fine out the back of the shop. It's delivery day for flour and sugar but she'll sleep through anything that child!"

The smell of dust and rats permeated through the air, but I wasn't going to be fussy about that. Thankfully the cats kept the rats under control and were nocturnal, so no action was happening until Bill arrived in the truck with the vegetables.

The truck coming in the distance seemed to be creating thicker dust than usual and its roar seemed more ferocious. I watched as I stood outside the shop and saw Bill's face as he pulled up near the woodheap at the back. He was upset which concerned me.

"Is everything all right?" I called out as he leapt out of the driver's seat.

He rushed in through the doorway and I followed. "Get some rags and old towels from the wash-house, Flo. There's been an accident. Poor Yufong's cut his hand and there's so much blood I don't know if his finger is still there or not."

By the lines of worry across Yufong's forehead and that tight-lip grimace I knew so well, I understood why Bill was concerned. Yufong held his injured hand, but bright red blood oozed through his fingers and dripped onto the seat.

"No worry, Mrs. I all right," but the look on his face told a different story. Mrs Mason ran out of the shop with towels and hessian bags, bustling her way through bags of flour and sugar. "Open the door wide, Love, so I can put these towels to good use."

She wrapped up his whole hand and half way up his arm despite weak protests from Yufong, who was clearly in a lot of pain. "Bill, if you drive to the nurse's post, then I think it's our day for a nurse to be on duty. You tend to Yufong, and I'll unload these veges from the back," and with that she hoisted herself up onto the back of the truck. I took the boxes from the truck as she passed them to me and put them onto the ground. I could see that this truck had to get moving quickly before Yufong lost any more blood. Within minutes Bill and the truck were gone and thick dust was left in its place.

"I think we need a cuppa after all that excitement," said Mrs Mason giving me a wink as she shuffled past, the sweat making a wet mark on her back. I think I was still in a bit of shock as the cup of tea arrived from Mrs Mason, with little Kathleen and Moreen in tow. It was not the first time I had marvelled at how children just accepted whatever was happening around them. For them, Daddy had just come and gone; this was part of their usual day. Their beautiful little faces were totally unaware of the near calamity.

My day continued with pies coming and going from my trolley, but I was anxious to get home and ask Bill about Yufong's injury. Some of the workers gave me their washing and others left ironing with Mrs Mason so this could be done when I arrived home from the road after selling the pies. How I wished there were some trees to provide shade but relief from the heat only came when the fierce sun's rays ceased to beat down on us. The sand was hot, but my shoes were standing up to harsh daily trudging along a track. The glare, too, was a hazard to endure. Hardly a day passed without me comparing this landscape to Ireland, where the smell and feel of dampness was ever present.

That night as the cool breeze blew through the house, I asked Bill about Yufong. "He's pretty lucky the nurse was there at the medical post and not away in Point Peron. She gave him a whiff of ether and put some stitches in. Then our towels were used to wrap around the bandage to try to keep it clean. He's a pretty brave man. Poor bugger. I'm not really sure how it happened. When I saw him, he was cutting his cabbages out in the field and then I heard him screaming. I shouted out to him but he was just jibbering away and I couldn't make any sense of what he said."

"Oh dear, I don't suppose he could understand you either, but it was pretty clear he was distressed."

The slippery slope between life and death raised its head again for me as I became acutely aware of how my little ones would suffer should any accident befall them. I was not good with the look and smell of blood. I was pleased to do the washing after dinner as a distraction and when I hung out shirts and trousers, I felt the comfort of the cool sea breeze. The scrubbing on the washing board always made me tired but that night I went to bed seeing Yufong's

face in my mind as he said, "I all right, Mrs." I was always amazed at how Bill could cope with blood but even he had been concerned about Yufong. Little did I know at that stage, just how much blood Bill was going to have to cope with in the not so distant future.

A letter from Audrey cheered me up when I recognised the familiar handwriting on the envelope as I sorted through the mail delivered to the shop. As I embarked on my daily pie run, with the hope of some washing along the way, I looked forward to the time when I could savour my letter and read it at leisure. With the waterbag swinging along beside us, Kathleen and Moreen took turns to pour out some water to provide a break in our walk. They tried to see who could see a truck first so we could make our base alongside it and use it for shade and coolness. They picked up sticks to draw in the sand and we would collect them to take home for our fire in the kitchen each night. I was mindful of snakes and last night's restless sleep put me on full alert for any danger. But the day passed uneventfully and soon it was time to go home, collect Heather and prepare for the evening.

"Come on, Kathleen. See if you can carry in some water in your billycan. Then we can boil our veges for your dinner. Moreen can carry in some sticks for the stove," and so this was a pattern for the unfolding of our days in 1930.

Chapter Ten

Christmas is Coming

The summer seemed to be settling in early as we looked forward to Christmas, and the wind seemed to blow relentlessly and swirled all the gum tree leaves around so they crunched under foot. I had just returned on the bus from Fremantle and it was close to tea time. With three small children, I was feeling tired, just like they were, but I lugged myself inside and fell into the nearest chair. Sweat ran down my back, but it was no good succumbing to the luxury of rest. I staggered up and began dinner preparations.

"Daddy, Daddy, we've been shopping. Mummy bought some things for Christmas," shouted Kathleen excitedly as Bill walked through the door.

"That's good. And what about little Heather and Moreen? Eh, what did you do today? Did you have a ride on the bus? Who helped Mummy carry some bags?"

The children adored their father, and who wouldn't? He was strong and handsome, with a summer tan developing on his arms and face. "Here's a letter from Audrey and George on the farm. Shall I open it now or wait until after dinner?"

He let the letter drop onto the wooden table and then went to wash before dinner, with three little ones tagging along behind. I could hear him splashing in the wash-house, ensuring that he used the rain water sparingly, just in case it was some time before the rain came to replenish our supplies in the tank. We tried to eat dinner before dark as the candles were another thing to add to our supply list from Mrs Mason. Bill wiped his face slowly and let the coolness run down his neck. It had been a long day driving the supply truck and now it was time to do the accounts for the end of November. I felt sorry for him as bookwork was a struggle.

As he sat down I passed him the letter to, hopefully, cheer him up.

"Flo, listen to this," said Bill as he read the letter from Williams. "George and Audrey are travelling to Perth to buy a new car. Well, it's not a new one but a secondhand one. And listen to this! They will drive it here on Christmas Day and spend Christmas night with us! We can have a drive in a car! How does that sound, Kathleen? What a magnificent Christmas present that will be!"

Imagine driving a car!

Normally Bill hated Christmas but now a car was coming, that was different. That night we sat outside and enjoyed the coolness of the air and the feeling of comfort knowing that the children were asleep and safe.

"Gosh, Flo, just imagine if we had remained in Ireland. At least we don't have to endure all those cold days leading up to Christmas."

I took off my apron, rubbed my feet into the sand and also thought of the times we'd had in Ireland where all we could think about was avoiding chilblains and keeping warm.

As I went to bed that night I fell asleep easily only to be awakened the next morning by the sea gulls screeching on our tin roof as they slid down noisily time and time again. I was pleased they didn't disturb the children who were lucky enough to sleep through all kinds of disturbance. Like me, they were exhausted each night. Sometimes Bill took them on his delivery run around the district and, with Christmas approaching, the store became quite busy. It was a relief to see him drive off in the truck as he drove to Fremantle each day to pick up supplies from the warehouse and then take goods to individuals. Bags of sugar and flour were delivered all around to local households, including Yufong's.

The roads were bumpy and dusty, but this didn't deter the children from sleeping. When Bill took them, it gave me a chance to catch my breath and continue the chores without interruption. When I knew he was delivering to Yufong's place it made me remember the time when poor Yufong cut his hand. I remembered how the blood ran between his fingers and how quickly death could snatch us up into his claws. Regularly a feeling of relief flooded through me and my mothering instinct was never far from the surface. We had all battled our own personal demons and I suspected Yufong and his family suffered more than most. His difficulty in speaking English, I could see, was a huge handicap for his whole family but his children were good workers and very kind to each other.

Like us, they were new arrivals who settled on a piece of land and soon his farm became a happy home. After a few years it was accepted that this was Yufong's place and his job was to grow vegetables in exchange for goods from Mrs Mason's shop. Somehow, he had acquired a rain water tank and some buckets so then his vegetables began growing. He now had half a dozen kids who spoke a mixture of Chinese and English and sometimes it was less trouble to deal with the children when it was time for barter or payment. Somehow, they were easier to understand and didn't wave their arms around trying to convey meaning. I had a real respect and admiration for Yufong and his family as they were enveloped into our community.

The day finished as Bill returned to the shop ready to unload and count out the day's takings, whether it was currency or goods. Sometimes he would encounter Bill or Eric, who drove the Pinjarra truck, with dairy and meat, and they would help each other. With little girls still sleeping in the truck, the sound of movement of heavy bags would fill the air. The grunts and groans of heavy labour indicated that the men were at work so Mrs Mason and I would stay inside out of the way! If Bill was on his own, we would venture out ready to lend a hand for the unloading or shifting of big heavy bags into the dedicated place in the shed.

"Who is waiting for Father Christmas?" Mrs Mason called into the truck and instantly the children were awake. She had shown them pictures of Father Christmas in the snow, painfully aware that this simply didn't make sense. All the children knew was that on a certain day, they would wake up to find a present at the end of their bed. I picked them up out of the truck and they walked with me across the road. We picked up wood from our wood pile and prepared to light the stove and begin our cooking. The heat didn't stop the daily fires from being lit each night as the wood stoves were essential for cooking. Candles were our tools for lighting and soon the darkness would envelope us all and allow slumber to sooth our souls in preparation for another day ahead.

Chapter Eleven

A New Car

"Mummy, look what Father Christmas gave me. He left a ball," squealed Kathleen as soon as the first light peeped through the window.

"And he left me a dolly," joined in Moreen.

They were very excited and so began the tradition of Christmas for the Brown family. I had been frugal in my shopping for the children, and for Heather I had sown a little dress, just to ensure that no-one missed out. I was used to spending on bare necessities only to ensure we had enough to eat. The poor men on the road looking for work was an image that never completely left my mind and I had seen enough poverty in Ireland to last me a life-time. I was mindful, too, that Bill's truck-driving for Mrs Mason was precarious at best. Still, I managed to save some money from my washing, ironing and pie-selling. I don't know why but I decided not to share this information with Bill.

The smell of toast cooking jerked me away from my reverie and took me back to the moment in our kitchen where we had to manage the day-to-day activities, such as breakfast.

"Right-oh, you lot. Let's go outside and wait for a new car to arrive. If you see some dust coming and hear the hum of an engine, then it could be Audrey and George. Go and clean your teeth first and then come to the front."

Bill hurried to the front of the house to begin his watch, as the sun beat down hard on his head and sea gulls screeched loudly in their normal madness. Gulls landed on our roof regularly and slid down, like it was part of their game. It seemed like they were also enjoying Christmas morning, despite the heat and the long day ahead. As for Mrs Mason and her boys, they were coming for dinner, so we could be a big family with all the merriment that goes with it. This was our first Christmas to be celebrated with special food, presents and visitors.

Soon, we could see some dust and then we heard a hum. "Here they come!" shouted the children and sure enough George and Audrey arrived in their new car.

The children had raced ahead and Bill and I waited with excitement as cars were such a rarity in our lives, but here was one pulling up just near us. We were so pleased to see our visitors, as well as seeing the car stopping just near our front gate. I touched the shiny steel and it felt hot and we feasted our eyes on the car for ages. The three-year-old car had been purchased for a special price of one hundred and fifty pounds, brand new ones being worth one hundred and sixty-nine pounds and ten pence. As I poked my head inside, the grey upholstery look so luxurious and the seats looked so comfortable.

A journalist of the day had described the car as *"much improved over its predecessors. The body has better lines, is more comfortable and more convenient in every way. The scuttle merges into the bonnet in a much more graceful manner than did that of the old model, whilst a better type of windscreen and hood are fitted. The body is fitted with four doors so that the driver does not have to squeeze past his front seat passengers while entering or leaving the car."*

I liked the way the seats were positioned low in the car and Audrey looked so little sitting in her seat. The canvas hood would keep off the sun and rain so that driving in any weather conditions would be comfortable. My heart beat with excitement as I anticipated a ride in it later in the day.

"Come inside and cool off. Let's have some time together so we can hear all your news. Actually, your news is right outside looking very grand near our house. What will passers-by have to say about this? Bill, they will think you've robbed a bank!

"Kathleen and Moreen, come inside now. Bring little Heather with you when you come. Later you can play in a bucket of water."

They loved doing this and now that Heather was walking and talking, she too, could join in the fun. It made easy entertainment and a bucket of water each day could be spared.

The afternoon was spent ensuring the wood stove was hot enough for our chicken and pork cooking. We had collected enough wood and Jim and Ron always brought home wood from their building sites and the children loved carrying in the small pieces. No-one was exempt from work! With the cooking smells emanating from the kitchen, we could then think about a ride in the car. Jim and Ron were first to have a ride, followed by Bill and Mrs Mason. Then it was my turn to endure total luxury, with the children, who squealed with pleasure as we drove along. I loved the glass for the windscreen and the canvas at the sides. I felt like a queen. Although new models would be coming out, and the newspapers often wrote about different model cars, nothing could surpass this feeling of beating the wind in my race along the road out past Yufong's place. I hoped he could see me, but he and his family would be inside their tent, escaping the heat. It was Christmas of 1931 and I was 31 years old, and feeling on top of the world.

"The colour is Imperial Buff," George called out. "There are three colours in this model - Empire Grey and Cobalt Blue are the others." I didn't care what colours there were. I was in heaven, speeding along the dusty track with the wind in my hair.

As we sat enjoying the coolness of the evening after our big dinner the talk turned to our futures. "Well," said Mrs Mason, "with those big poles out there we will soon have electricity in the shop. No more Tilley lights and candles at night. No more lugging kerosene all the time. Just imagine that. You, too, will have lights in your house! Perth has had lights for ages and now we can join the new age."

Jim and Ron, too, were delighted. "You'll still need kero for your fridges, Mum. Okay, now, Bill. What is your news?"

"I've a new job! Some bloke asked me if I did any book-keeping and knew anything about numbers so I told him he was looking at the right person! Then he asked me if I would join the crew at the Commonwealth Bank in Rockingham. Can you imagine that? I'd love a new car to drive to work, George! Sorry Mrs Mason, you'll need to get a new driver but there are plenty of blokes out there looking for work."

"Never mind," said Mrs Mason. "Ron can do that. His work has slowed down and he needs more hours. One needs to be grateful in these uncertain times. Just so long as we can share it all around. Jim's work continues well with all these new houses being built. And I guess they, too, will be on the power so I'd better slow down with the candle making and Tilley lights. Don't want old stock. It's too expensive to keep it all lying around out the back. You two boys can do a stock-take and tidy up tomorrow. Just make sure we have enough waterbags and keep that ice-man happy. We need our ice, don't we, Flo? And now, Flo, what's your news? Are we having pudding after that beautiful meal?" She laughed as she said it – the plum pudding waiting in the kitchen came right from her larder.

"My news?" I thought very carefully before I spoke as I wasn't quite sure how my news would be taken. I had been feeling particularly tired in recent times and during the last week I worked out the reason. With full breasts and tight skirts, my suspicions became reality when I counted back the months.

"Bill, we are going to have another baby." He took the news better than I had expected but perhaps the alcohol has eased his reasoning. Audrey was delighted but I felt that she was working hard to cover her true feelings of being childless. "And if we have a boy we'll call him George. If we have a girl, we'll call her Audrey. I've counted the months and I think he or she will be born in May. This will be a winter baby, Bill. That's a sign of good luck. This year, 1932, is going to be a good one. Let's drink a toast to us all. New cars, new jobs and new babies. Oh yes and new lights! We all have a lot to be happy about."

I wasn't sure if a winter baby was a sign of good luck or not. I just made that up on the spot as it seemed a good thing to say. With three other children, I would need a good bit of luck going my way.

Chapter Twelve

The Commonwealth Bank

I watched Bill and Kathleen leave, the bus slowly pulling away from the bus stop on its way along the bumpy road. Bill's new job began soon after Christmas and it meant a bus ride into town each day, luckily leaving in time to take Kathleen to school. I waved goodbye to them, painfully aware that Kathleen would be upset.

Bill wasn't really that tolerant and her crying annoyed him, so he looked out the window and watched the seagulls and the sandhills as they caressed the hot landscape. Riding along like this gave him time to think and often his mind slipped back into times when he was a young man without family ties. Oh, they were the days when he could do what he wanted and didn't have to think about kids and their needs. However, he was a responsible man, so he knew that, when the bus stopped, he would have to walk Kathleen to school and then take a short walk to the Post Office/Commonwealth Bank.

The middle-aged lady always greeted him as he walked into the building and this, too, annoyed Bill. Why did she always have to be so chirpy when, on some mornings, it clearly wasn't a good morning? He grimaced and smiled woodenly as he stepped into business mode for the day. The post office and the bank operated in the same building in downtown Rockingham. Barney, a small man with horn-rimmed glasses, as one may expect, was the bank boss.

Bill began by opening the shutters and ensuring the balance from the previous day was up to date. With pen and paper ready, he was now able to focus on being civil to customers who came through the door. With his eye on the clock all day, he always looked forward to lunch time when he could walk down to the park, open his paper bag and eat his sandwich. His waterbag was usually warm by this stage, but he drank from it anyway. The afternoons seemed to drone on and the odd fly seemed to be a nuisance as it, too, fought for its existence. Slowly but surely, each day arrived at 4 o'clock and he made his way to the heavy door and departed for the day.

Kathleen would be waiting for him in the park and always ran towards him through the shade of the old trees. She was a lively child and ran into her father's arms as if each day had been an endurance for her too.

The noisy, dusty bus ride home was interspersed with Kathleen drinking from his waterbag and her aim each day was to ensure it was empty before Mrs Mason's shop came into sight.

"Why does it have to be empty, Kathleen?" asked Bill as he

looked down on her sweet face.

"Then it's lighter for you to carry," she answered in her high-pitched child-like voice. She was the eldest and had developed all the leadership skills that came with this position in the family. Now, there would be another soon, he dwelt. And it hadn't been planned. None of them were planned but they were a bit of fun when they grew out of that baby stage. This job in the bank wasn't really what he liked but he was acutely aware that any job was better than nothing.

It was 1933 and the Depression, as it was later known, was starting to hit countries hard. The Wall Street crash happened in 1929 and that seemed to signal the beginning of hard times for the industrialised world. Soon unemployment would rise to 21% here and then it would climb to 32% of Australians looking for work. There was talk about a stock market crash, but no-one seemed sure about the details. The only thing folk could be sure of was there were more men walking the streets asking for work. Bill had made up his mind he wasn't going to be one of them. He would regularly glance at the news headlines on Mrs Mason's newspapers to check out what was happening.

He soon grew tired of bad economic news and started instead to follow the English cricket team on the 'Bodyline' Ashes tour with some fellow called Harold Larwood bowling the ball straight at the chap who was batting. There was talk of being a bad sport, but Bill thought that if anyone was mad enough to stand on a cricket pitch, then a batsman had to expect a cricket ball coming from any direction. He didn't see how it was bad form at all, but he was cynical enough to know that journalists had to keep inventing news for readers. They were tired of reading about the opening of some bridge in Sydney – a city so far away. Readers were certainly tired of reading about the formation of the Australian Broadcasting Commission! Anything to distract the Australian people from the harsh realities of life without a pay-packet coming in each week! Then his sight was directed to his bus stop ahead and the creaking, shaking, rattling of the old bus engine came to an end. He could see his family waiting in the shade for his arrival.

I was uncomfortable with this pregnancy, but baby Audrey arrived as planned, in the middle of May with the minimum of fuss. It was almost like she knew she had to enter the world quietly and then remain close to her sisters for survival and comfort. With three older siblings, all close in age, Audrey would grow up to be a real help for me. To gain my attention, she was the helper while the others amused themselves with childhood activities. Her sense of responsibility developed from an early age. She was the one who would do the fetching; she was the one who demanded least attention. It was no wonder that I thought her a 'dream' child. At this stage, as if by some intuition, Audrey seemed to know that her time as a baby was going to be very short lived. She idealised her sisters who all wanted to treat her like a new toy and Audrey adored their attention. She rode in the back of bikes where someone had put her; she laid on the blanket when her sisters grew tired of the games. She fitted into the clothes outgrown by the others when there was no time or money for extras. I was still busy selling pies on the road and doing other people's washing and ironing. Lucky there wasn't a Depression at the Brown household in Safety Bay Road! There were children everywhere and noise all over the place, but no-one was hungry or lonely.

"Bill, can you give the ice man a hand?" Mrs Mason called from across the road as the daily truck arrived with its ice on the back ready for deliveries. Blocks of ice were shunted into the Coolgardie safes at the shop and into Bill's Coolgardie safe on the back verandah, where it was out of the sun and ideally located to ensure that food could be kept as cool as possible. Not much food was wasted with all the mouths to feed but Bill was adamant some food was put out the front on a table near the shop so men looking for work would not go hungry. He was a generous, though impatient man, who would always instill a sense of responsibility into his kids. He watched the ice-man leave and counted the gears the truck went through before it reached maximum speed along the pot-holed, dusty track. He missed driving the truck for Mrs Mason, but knew that her sons needed looking after in terms of employment and the bank job paid more. He had to be contented. Besides, someone had to take Kathleen to school and soon there would be Moreen.

He tried hard not to look too far ahead, and had learnt early in his life that he shouldn't expect too much.

"Take each day as is comes, son," his mum had said to him, and he marvelled at how words like this seem to stay in one's mind, and remembered them often. At the age of thirty-three he had many more times ahead in his life to remember them again and again.

Chapter Thirteen

A Surprise for the Family

"There, there, Love," cooed Mrs Mason. "You'll manage." Once again Mrs Mason's embrace gave me comfort as she played mother to me.

"I'm thirty-two and I should be able to cope but I just feel so upset," I reasoned but my heart wasn't telling me that. "How did it happen?" I pleaded in desperation.

"I'm sure we both know the answer to that," she smugly replied as she began to go about her daily business of opening the old, big doors to the shop. Her rational response made me smile.

The sun crept in to signal a new day and slowly the sounds of life began taking their course. "Oh well, a new baby will be here in the new year. I thought that if I was breast feeding then, I couldn't get pregnant."

"You'll manage because you always do. You'll have to stop the pie-making and just continue to do laundry and ironing. I know! Why don't we use the shop as a depot and that may even create more business for me?"

I tried to smile as I left the shop, forever grateful to this woman who had her own problems. Her husband had died when the two boys were young and here she was managing a shop, and a profitable one at that. I marvelled at her resilience and tried to see life as she painted it. That wasn't easy, so to help me through the moment I allowed myself some time where I could wallow in my misery and helplessness by walking briefly along the beach, listening to the waves. It was November, so the weather was pleasant as I sat at the edge of the water, allowing it to massage my feet and acknowledging that time could ease my soul. I wasn't going to think of Ireland; that became remote now as this was my new life, even though it seemed over-whelming at present.

Just a very short distance away three fishermen continued a struggle with their fishing net, trying their hardest to ensure they trapped as many fish as possible in their net. I knew their routine – by ten o'clock one of them would be in the shop trying to negotiate a payment in either cash or goods. As I listened to them speaking to each other in a foreign tongue, babbling and talking over each other all the time, I thought that they, too, were having a difficult life. Imagine not being able to speak the language, I thought. I knew there was a Chinese settlement now, at Yufong's place, where more tents had been erected. I could understand why they all lived together, and the realisation dawned of how interdependent we all were, trying to eke out a living in a land away from home. I wondered which one of them knew enough English to negotiate with Mrs Mason.

As they walked past me one of them smiled his toothy smile, nodded his head and said something unintelligible so I answered a quiet greeting to him, knowing that we had connected somehow in this land of togetherness, despite the disparity of our backgrounds.

As I entered our home, the sounds of children greeted me, and I knew my time for any kind of day-dreaming had come to an end for now. With Kathleen and Bill on the bus, I was left with three little ones, who thankfully played on their own. They loved playing in the sand and bush close by and when I gave them some water from our limited supply they were in heaven. Each morning water from the melted ice that kept our food cool each day, provided a new purpose for the children's play. However, it would be coming to an end soon as our Coolgardie safe was going to be replaced by a kerosene refrigerator, which was to be our family Christmas present.

My sewing machine, too, was useful for Christmas presents for the children who were now fully aware of this phenomenon called Santa Claus. As I looked at baby Audrey, who was only four months old, I felt a massive surge of responsibility swell up and I knew my time for self-pity was over. She needed me; the others needed me, and so too did Bill and Kathleen, rattling away on that rickety old bus each day. Moreen would join them after Christmas and at that point I decided I was too tired to have a shopping  day in Perth; clothes, a refrigerator and a new baby were our Christmas presents for 1932.

"Oh no," moaned Bill when I told him in the privacy of our bedroom that night. I knew he wouldn't be happy but then again, nor was I.

"That makes two of us. We'll just have to deal with it. I know you don't really like working in the bank Bill but don't, whatever you do, give it up."

He had been complaining incessantly recently and that gave me cause for concern. He was also growing increasingly impatient with the children and his dissatisfaction at work he cited as the cause for his irritability.

"It's another mouth to feed. I thought we weren't having any more."

I didn't try to negate his unreasonableness; I just let him rant. I had learnt long ago that I couldn't change how he felt and I'm sure that's why I leant on Mrs Mason for emotional support. We both went to sleep that night very unhappy and I was just hopeful the children hadn't heard any of our conversation.

The day before Christmas our refrigerator arrived on a big truck. It was very exciting as Mrs Mason was also purchasing one for the shop. It was almost evening when the truck manoeuvred itself around corners to enable some serious grunt work to take place as men performed their work and shifted the fridges (as they came to be called) into their positions. I was glad Bill was home to give him a welcome distraction, and physical work seemed to be a pleasure for him. He seemed to like, what he termed, 'men's work'.

I cringed as I realised that he saw his job in the bank as something other than 'men's work' – not quite women's work, but physical work defined his idea of masculinity, so it was with some concern that I worried about what the new year would bring.

"Righto, you kids, get all those containers out and put them near the fridge," called out Bill between grunts.

The shop man had told her to ensure they kept the fridge working for twenty-four hours prior to any cooling to maximise efficiency but I didn't want to distract Bill. I just let him organise the children into their roles of who would do what. He seemed to like doing that and the children loved it. The two men who drove the delivery truck looked exhausted as they wheeled the fridge onto our back verandah and they grunted with each push as our Christmas present was moved into position against the wall. After paying the workmen we were free to admire our new fridge, trying our hardest not to open the door and let the cool air escape.

"Gosh, with electric lights one year and a new fridge another year, Bill, we are just so fortunate. I feel so lucky," and for a moment the thoughts about a new baby drifted away to a safe place in my mind.

The humming noise was quite loud but that signalled our good fortune and went some way to softening the screech of the sea gulls, which became rather annoying at times. The children were delighted and loved touching the cold metal and began singing with the humming noise. Bill and I looked at each other and smiled; it was always like a new day with the delights that children found in the banal.

"You gotta love them, Flo," Bill laughed. "Don't worry too much about this new baby. I'm getting used to the idea and hey, maybe it will be a boy. Then I can teach him how to trap rabbits."

With a mention of rabbits, Kathleen and Moreen began pestering their father to take them on his rounds. The long days allowed Bill time in the early evening to trap rabbits so, with some old fish heads in his billy, he called them to follow him as he proceeded towards the back of the yard.

"Daddy, can I put a fish head in a trap?"

He had made the mistake of allowing this once and now the children wanted to do this all the time, but it was too dangerous. I had been angry when Kathleen told me that her hand had been inside a rabbit trap, so I threatened to keep them home if they ever did that again.

They were away until dark, which was their signal to return home. It was difficult to see sticks in the way along the path and, having three rabbit traps, the children were interested enough only to maintain an enthusiasm for the half hour or so. Bill curtailed their urge to run as he was not keen to incur my wrath if someone hurt themselves and, of course, he was responsible for them when they were hunting rabbits. He was always pleased when they arrived home and he could relinquish them back into my care.

The next evening they would check the traps and thus measure their success as hunters, and this constituted the basis of many of the children's games.

Chapter Fourteen

Beulah joins the Family

Beulah joined the family in March – a cool time of the year. This meant the weather was kinder and reminded us both of Scotland, where weather conditions were a critical factor in planning holidays – these were a rare event when we were young. Bill's family travelled to the southern part of England one year, to a place called Beulah. The trees were green, the grass was lush, and the sun actually shone! The wind blew softly, unlike the wind in Safety Bay. He couldn't remember a great deal about the place called Beulah, but he remembered that he liked the word. I was indifferent about a name so when Bill suggested Beulah, that's what it became.

I knew Bill worried about how I would cope and, indeed, I worried too. My main concern was the close age gap between Beulah and baby Audrey who was yet to turn one. I was lucky Audrey was a very contented baby and when she cried Heather or Moreen would tend to her.

"Flo, that's going to happen with this baby too. You just wait and see."

I wasn't convinced and that annoyed Bill. He didn't really understand women and now he had a whole house full of them. I think he was secretly disappointed when the baby hadn't been a boy but, after five girls, what else could he expect?

"I was hoping that it was Michael who would join us, Flo," he said one night. As sure as anything there weren't going to be any more babies and he was aware that he had to work hard to ensure that the family didn't increase.

As time went on, Bill grew to dislike his job more and more. That lady who greeted him each morning had left but, in her place, was another woman who was just as bad. He really had to discipline himself and say nothing offensive, and he quickly realised that holding his tongue and being civil to everyone who walked through the door was the part of his job he hated most. Each day became more and more about watching the clock until it was time to leave so he could walk to the park for Moreen and Kathleen. His life seemed like a ticking time bomb and Bill was later to learn how challenging life could be but for now he just went through the motions each day.

The months and weeks seemed endless with the daily grind. It wasn't the numbers and the bookwork he hated, it was dealing with stupid people. They would come in and look around, then ask dumb questions, so Bill knew it was only a matter of time until he was irritable enough to tell them a few home truths.

It happened one day when he was least expecting it, when he thought his depression and anger were under control.

"Can I please cash this cheque?" asked an elderly woman as she peered up from under her glasses and well-worn hat.

"ID please," Bill asked drearily.

The woman, looking fatigued and hot, riffled to the bottom of her handbag. "I can't seem to find it. Hmmm, I think I left it home."

"Well, what are you coming in here for? You're expecting me to believe you? No ID, no cash." Bill knew his voice sounded angry, but he didn't care. If he was reasonable he would have understood that she could have easily left her paperwork at home; she looked so vulnerable, not like a thief, but Bill didn't feel patient that day. He'd arrived at work late, then chastised by Barney so now he felt totally ambivalent about raising his voice to a frail old woman. "You'll have to go home and get it."

Soon the woman was crying, and her sniffling was so loud that Barney left his chair and approached the back of the counter.

"What's happening, Mrs Green?" Barney asked irritably as he looked at Bill. A coldness passed over Bill as he tried to reach that thread of decency that he knew lay deep within him.

"No ID, Sir, no cash. Isn't that our rule?"

"Of course it is, Bill, but this is Mrs Green, not some thug who just walked in off the street."

"Listen Barney, you make up the rules, so I can carry them out. Then what happens? You step in and flaunt the rules. Rules are rules, mate. Who am I to say which rules apply to which customer or not?"

Bill knew he was in dangerous territory, but he was sick of this little upstart thinking he was the boss. Here he was kowtowing to Mrs Green just because Barney knew who she was, and he didn't. Nothing wrong with obeying rules!

He felt his heart racing and felt like banging something, but he stood his ground. "So, Barney, is this rule no longer a rule? I'm only asking a question."

Meanwhile Mrs Green stood there, snivelling.

As the seconds passed, it seemed like hours.

"Mrs Green, how much is the cheque made out for?" asked Barney in that obsequious little voice he used only on women.

Bill fumed as he knew this was no longer about cashing cheques. This was about two men flexing muscle and this made him furious. Soon he saw a twenty-pound note pass over the counter and of course, she took it and just put it in her bag!

Bill looked at the cheque and felt like tearing it up. He realised his knuckles were clenched, and his chest was barely managing to contain his fast-beating heart. He looked up in time to see her leaving the bank, still snivelling, a bent over little figure stepping carefully in case she should fall.

Barney followed her out and, on her departure, he heard Barney click the door and lock it.

"Bill you can't treat valued customers like that. How many times have I told you? Why did that make you so angry?" Barney sounded quite reasonable and Bill knew what he said was right, but he knew about rules and he liked rules. "Bill, I really think you should look for another job that might be better suited for you. I can see that customer service is just not your thing. Look, how about you leave quietly and I'll give you a good reference for your next job. What do you say to that?"

Bill's anger subsided, and he knew what Barney said made sense. This job wasn't for him. This wasn't a man's job. He couldn't be nice to little old ladies all day and bend … no, break … the rules for them. He thought once again. Rules are rules but he remained quiet while he dug deep for some composure.

He thought for some time before he formed his response, aware of the gravity of the situation. He knew Barney was breaking rules so therefore he was in the right. This made his anger dissipate slightly. After what seemed to be an eternity, he simply said, "Yep, I quit."

He was surprised at how calm he was when he gathered up his belongings and put them in the bag he brought to work each day. As he left the building he didn't say a word or look back. He could hear Barney calling out something about coming back for his reference, but he had other things on his mind now. He was going to the pub where real men gathered.

As the amber fluid ran down his throat he felt a calmness run through him and he felt his muscles relax and his knuckles unclench. God, that Barney was a loser, and he felt glad he wouldn't have to deal with him again. He wasn't even sure that he would go back for his reference.

As he ordered his second drink, he suddenly remembered he had to meet his children in the park and catch the bus home with them. Oh well, just a few drinks here won't hurt.

"How am I going to tell my wife?"

Deep in conversation with a stranger, Bill avoided going home for as long as possible. Deep down he knew he would have to muster up all the courage in the world to tell me what had happened and he knew he would incur my wrath and all the ferocity that went with it.

Audrey and Beulah, 1950.

Chapter Fifteen

Letters to Audrey

21 Safety Bay Road
Safety Bay
5/3/1934

Dear Audrey

I do hope that all is well with you and George. Things are not good for me and, in fact, I am quite desperate. I will cut to the chase as quickly as I can and then I will fill you in with details. Bill quit his job in the bank and is now out of work.

He did not even tell me at first, continuing to catch the bus to Rockingham each morning with the children. One day I asked him if he could take little Audrey to buy some shoes in his lunch hour and he agreed to this. The plan was that I would put Audrey on the bus and tell the driver that Bill would meet him at the other end of the line. The driver had assured me that this was a good idea. I felt comfortable enough despite the idea of Audrey being only a toddler and these shoes were to be her first shoes. It should have been an exciting day and it was in the beginning. Around two o'clock a bus driver knocked on our door with little Audrey in his arms, sobbing her heart out. Basically Bill had not turned up to meet the bus! Naturally I thought that something had happened to him but I had to wait until later in the day. You can imagine my dismay.

When Bill arrived home later in the day with Kathleen and Moreen I confronted Bill. I have never had such a dreadful argument with him. He simply went to the pub while the children went to school and pretended that he was at work. I don't know how long this has been going on for!

Oh Audrey, you can imagine my anger at his deception! I hate to ask a favour of you but do you have any work for him? Men are continuing to walk the streets looking for work and Bill refuses to do that. I have read in the paper about the completion of the Sydney Harbour bridge and now all those men are looking for work, so apparently it is nationwide – this shortage of work. It is no different from the poverty in Ireland.

I continue to be very busy with the children, as you can imagine, and I am surprised to see how Kathleen and Moreen look after the little ones. They continue to surprise me and, really, they just act so grown up. Before all this happened, I was quite happy but now to make matters worse I think I am pregnant again. I haven't told Bill yet. I fear that could well be the last thing to make our lives a total disaster. As for money, I continue to take in washing and ironing, so I hope to be all right in that aspect. I continue to put some aside, with only me knowing, as I recognise the dark face of poverty and I don't want the children to see my desperation.

My very dear friend, I will sign off now. I must rouse myself as "it's Kathleen's birthday today". She is turning eight and growing up fast. Bill has killed one of our old chickens, so we will have roast dinner tonight.

Forever your best of friend,

Flo

21 Safety Bay Road
Safety Bay
5/3/1936

Dear Audrey

It is two years now since I wrote to you in total desperation and oh, I am so grateful. If I believed in God, I would thank you in my prayers, but you know the story on that one! Yes, I am much happier now and hopefully I can put that dark period aside. But do you know? It has gone so quickly that I can hardly remember much – I cannot supply a lot of news.

Fancy baby Pauline arriving on Heather's birthday! Now, of course, she is the baby now doing all the things that toddlers do. I found that this time I didn't worry. It was my seventh birth, so it went very easily and when I got home the children just did everything for her. As for her being a girl, well, after six girls a seventh seemed natural.

The absence of Bill seemed a bonus and I have become very independent, realising that life just continues. I thank you so much for taking Bill off my hands! I know that sounds a bit cheeky but at times he just created turmoil with his rules and regulations here at home. For these two years I just appreciate the fact that you gave him a roof over his head, even if it was a mattress in the cowshed, so please do not worry about not paying him. Just doing what you did really saved me. I know he likes manual work and being outside suits him best. I am sure that he did work hard chopping trees down and hopefully that has made your farm more productive.

Imagine you growing fruit trees now! That is a wonderful thing to do. Your cold winters are helpful for setting the fruit. The wind continues to blow relentlessly here and the sand continues to envelope us all the time. Mrs Mason's boys tell me not to complain about the wind as it is the driving force for our windmill, so our water supply is never in doubt. Jim and Ron put in a new rainwater tank last week, as our old one continued leaking. It is round – so unlike our old square one. It is just out the back so we do not have far to carry in our water. I cannot grow anything in the garden but our weekly supply of fruit and vegetables from Yufong continues in exchange for pies.

Dearest Audrey and George, thank you so much regarding this new job for Bill in Shenton Park. He will love being outdoors doing a milk delivery. It sounds like a dream come true. And a house is available too! I am very excited about our move and our fishermen friends want to buy our house here in Safety Bay. I have not told the children yet and I am concerned about leaving my dearest friend Mrs Mason. She has been a mother to me – and she continues to be so. This will be a great wrench. Also, it will be an adjustment for children and school. I wonder if I will still take in washing? I am pleased that it will not happen until after winter. I have really grown accustomed to winters by the ocean, with the specific sounds and smells. Nevertheless, you are so kind and generous in your attentions to our family. Words cannot express the gratitude I feel for helping us out in our difficult times. As for Bill joining us again after his stay with you, it will be an adjustment for us all.

I remain as always, your beloved friend

Flo.

Chapter Sixteen

70 Aberdare Road – Shenton Park

When we moved to Shenton Park I thought this was our new opportunity. Bill unpacked the furniture into the new house with relish, lifting all the heavy items into their place. He whistled as he strutted down the passage, his head held high as he looked forward to his future. He hadn't minded his work on the Williams' farm, in fact he quite liked it, but the lack of money meant the situation was only temporary. He didn't even think about money very much and I was aware that I was the one who held the family together, ever mindful that money, or lack thereof, was the difference between life and starvation. After our early life in Ireland, I didn't think this was over-reacting.

"Kathleen, watch it!" I heard Bill say as she tried to carry some clothes into the bedroom. He always seemed to be calling out to her and wondering why she couldn't be more careful. The others, of course, were outside playing their own games, but Kathleen always wanted to somehow get in the way.

"Bill, she's only trying to help."

I was aware I was taking Kathleen's side and knew I would have to adapt to appease Bill without offending our beloved eldest daughter, the one who always helped me. As the feisty one in the family, Kathleen wasn't offended by her father's reprimand and soon joined her sisters in their excitement of exploring the new back yard. The big expanse of grass went all the way to the chicken yard near the back fence and the toilet, thus providing lots of room for their games. The grass had a fresh smell and the jasmine flowers were new to the children. Around the side were neatly clipped privets that made a passageway near the path for the children's bikes so they could ride all around the house. The track between the toilet and the front door was the area deemed by the children to be theirs.

As evening approached, Bill looked anxiously up and down the tree-lined street awaiting a visit from his boss who had promised to call in with instructions for the job the next day. Soon a slight figure in the distance came within sight and Bill recognised him as a man of the cloth. This was Bill's cue to look away and start lighting his cigarette, but the other man was not so easily swayed by a lack of conventions and the usual reverence held for priests.

"Hello, good sir. I see you are moving in with your family," he said, uttering the obligatory official line as a way into this new family, who could be potential new parishioners.

The priest was accustomed to obsequious behaviours, but Bill was determined to make him sweat; he wasn't going to observe the usual niceties which accompanied such interactions with men who claimed to have a pathway to God. Bill wasn't going to elicit any conversation from him and I worked this out as I watched him through the curtains.

I called him inside. "Who was that?" I asked, unpacking boxes of clothes into drawers. I could feel the tension in the air and it made me uneasy.

"It's not someone you need to contend yourself with," Bill replied. "Just coz it's Easter they think they can come around here annoying the first person they see."

Still edgy with anger, he roused himself to think about the visit from his boss, Mr Reagan, and took himself off to sit on the back-verandah steps and wait for a knock on the door. He liked to watch the children playing and they knew he preferred to watch them rather than participate with them. He simply couldn't be bothered, but he enjoyed Heather and Moreen coming to sit either side of him, nudging close to him. Heather was a friendly child and Moreen adored her, simply adhering to all that Heather said.

Soon there was a loud knock on the front door and Bill prepared himself to be as social as Heather or Moreen in his interactions with Mr Reagan. The man entered the house in his working clothes and Bill took him to the front room. With his thumbs in his trousers, Bill nodded towards one of the well-worn chairs and soon the two men were comfortably seated ready for their work talk.

"Go down to the end of the street, heading east, so you arrive at the end of Aberdare Road. That's the depot and the stables where you'll find other blokes loading up for their milk run. Here is a map of where you'll be expected to go." Mr Reagan didn't waste any words, but Bill was attentive, listening carefully as if his life depended on it. Riding on a horse and cart was going to give him his newfound freedom and he wasn't going to muck it up.

He took the piece of screwed-up paper Mr Reagan removed from his pocket – this was his map for his milk run so he studied it carefully.

I entered the front room with a teapot and tea cups, saved only for special visitors so Mr Reagan felt that this was an auspicious occasion for us newcomers to Perth. Breathing steadily, my eyes rested on Bill in some newfound apprehension. This was going to work!

That night as we lay in bed, we talked about how this new venture was going to be good for the family. Bill knew the wrench from Mrs Mason had been serious for me and felt sympathetic. He knew he had messed up the bank job and now he had six children dependent upon him; he knew the future weighed heavily upon him. He was aware that I was doing it tough.

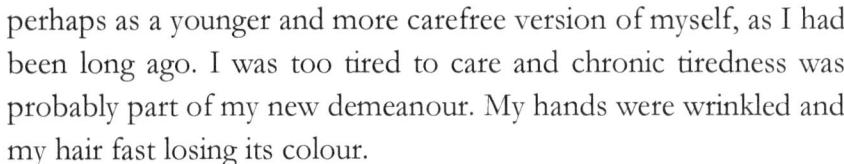

"Flo you've changed. I really hope you can be happier now I have paid work."

I knew he was looking at me in the half dark and mentally thinking of me perhaps as a younger and more carefree version of myself, as I had been long ago. I was too tired to care and chronic tiredness was probably part of my new demeanour. My hands were wrinkled and my hair fast losing its colour.

"You've still got those blue flashing eyes and those rosy cheeks, Flo," I heard him say as I drifted off to a deep sleep of exhaustion.

So, the era of living in Perth began and Safety Bay soon became a distant memory. Bill loved his new job and the children settled into their new life quickly.

Riding around the quiet streets of Shenton Park, along Stirling Highway and into Nedlands allowed Bill time to embrace the sounds of the horse clip-clopping along the bitumen surface. Pouring milk from large containers into small ones was second nature to him and he enjoyed life in the open, with the fresh air blowing in his face as the animals created their own momentum for him. He enjoyed looking after the horses at the end of each day, patting them on their heads as they ate their daily allowance of hay in the stables.

His job entailed cleaning water troughs and stables, but he was used to manual work. He reflected for a moment on his time in the bank when he had to endure fools each day and now he was thankful he could almost obliterate speaking from his working life. Any time others felt the urge to talk, he started whistling and looking away, realising this marked the end of any conversation others may feel the need to undertake. He was happy, and walking home each night allowed him to hear birds in the trees and listen to the domestic sounds happening as evening threatened to end each day, and separate it from the others in the process of life. Children playing, and the sounds of the odd train or vehicle intercepted his thoughts and turned his mind to the evening meal, wondering what smells would emanate from his new abode in Perth.

"I'm home, Flo," he called out as I reached into the oven for another meal to be served to the Brown clan!

Chapter Seventeen

The Move to Rivervale

I enjoyed living in Shenton Park but knew it was only temporary as our lease ran out in six months. I was just so thankful to Audrey and George for accommodating Bill on their farm but more importantly, they were instrumental in this new role on the milk run. If ever I had reason to believe in a god, then this was the time. This position of milk delivery and caring for horses really suited Bill and having an income was a lifeline, as I had just started dipping into our savings. I tried hard to be a saver, just like my mother, and I wasn't going to impart knowledge of our bank account balance to Bill, who was totally oblivious to the notion of saving. He lived in the moment, but I had six children to care for and here in the city it was going to be different and who knows how difficult.

Thankfully, I was spared the misery on men's faces as they asked for work at Mrs Mason's shop, though when I was behind the counter, it broke my heart to turn them away and hear them shuffle into the distance, dressed in the dishevelled clothes they had slept in the night before. The daily newspaper described unemployment as heading towards thirty percent but there in Safety Bay these men were the human face of it all. I missed Mrs Mason terribly and wept when I said my final good byes; now a different part of my life was beginning but it was a life, hopefully, where I could concentrate on being a mother instead of being a bread-winner. Perhaps Bill and I may even improve our relationship, which had become distant in recent times, and maybe my exhaustion would even subside. For the present though, I was going to focus on home and children and let

Bill take care of his own life, though I would take care of the weekly pay packet; it was lucky really that he left all that side to me and I wasn't going to spend a single penny more from our savings if I could help it.

I was so pleased that local fishermen, whose names I barely knew, bought our house from us in Safety Bay. They came into the shop each day with their wares and, of course, I was there to encounter anyone who lived on this earth with my bid to sell our house. It was rather fortuitous they were good savers too and could put their money straight into my bank account. They loved the idea of living near home, work and the shop. Now that we had a six-month lease on a house, and the money in the bank, we had time to look for our next family home.

After taking the eldest children to the local primary school, I would look at the local paper to investigate house sales. Actually, buying a newspaper was foreign for me as I was privy to newspapers in the Safety Bay shop! I also missed fresh rabbit for dinner and fresh vegetables from Yufong. The few thin-looking chickens in the back yard were remiss when it came to laying eggs and I suspected that some suburban night creature was growing fat at our expense. Bill was determined to look out for good firewood on his rounds and he was true to his word as the wood heap in the back yard was small and we knew it wouldn't last long.

It wasn't long before I identified a property on Great Eastern Highway that was for sale and within our price range. It was a red brick house with three bedrooms, so that weekend we made the journey across town to Rivervale to look at the house. With the old tee-tree hedge at the front along the brick fence and the huge leafy tree in the front yard, we were delighted. Bill, who was a talented drawer, sketched a picture of the house so he could show the children. I liked hearing a few cars on the road and it rather reminded me of Finaghy Road in Belfast. Growing used to the isolation of Safety Bay was something that had slowly crept up on me, but now I felt I had returned to the familiarity of civilisation.

240 Great Eastern Highway in Rivervale was our new address but it would be a few months before we could move in. The financial business between Real Estate agent, owner and tenant was due to be settled soon and the children loved Bill's drawing of our new home.

"Wasn't that Mrs Casey nice, Bill? And to think that she wants to see the children for afternoon tea next Sunday. How lucky are we to have a nice neighbour like that! I hope she turns out to be as loving as Mrs Mason." I was delighted with our good fortune and my spirits soared.

"Yes, she does seem okay. I'm glad her husband has the newspaper shop on the corner so I can get cigarettes and a newspaper for us each day. Flo, that can be your job! On second thoughts, perhaps Kathleen or Moreen can do that. They are old enough now to assume responsibility."

For Bill it was important that the children had jobs to do and I endorsed that idea. I was delighted too, that little Audrey helped me with Beulah and toddler Pauline, though they were getting older now and were starting to look after themselves.

Chapter Eighteen

Death of a Child

Our little Pauline left the world as silently as she had entered. I felt guilty because having a child, at the time of her birth, was the last thing in the world I had wanted, and now she was gone.

I sat quietly in my lounge chair and let the tears settle on my cheeks and made no attempt to hide them. I couldn't muster up any strength and I just wanted to wallow in my own world and my own pity. I didn't even care what the children did, said or felt – I was consumed in my own pain for my loss and guilt. I wondered what I would have felt if this child had been wanted but soon my stoic nature brought me back to reality and I knew I was creating my own artificial reality to alleviate my total anguish. I needed to be practical and realise that she had died of Pneumonia and there was nothing that I could have done to keep her cough subdued.

It took many years before I stopped hearing her cough at night as I would wake up and think she was still alive in my nightmares. If I'd been a religious person, I could have been comforted by thoughts of her reunion with her dead sister Flo, but I just didn't believe that, and so my pain continued until it dissipated into a perpetual sadness. It took many years to fade and I consoled myself with the thought that no mother really gets over the death of a child, particularly an unwanted one, as the guilt always lingers.

Our move into Rivervale had been difficult too as the tenant had refused to vacate the premises. We were so thankful to Mr Casey who liaised with a member of Parliament to manage his eviction. We managed to stay in Aberdare Road for a few extra weeks, but it was almost like the foreshadowing of a sinister event, as Pauline died soon afterwards. Ultimately it had been the warmth of another woman, this time Mrs Casey, who roused me from my mourning, and the other children's good nature that pulled me from my stupor and made me see purpose in life again.

Thankfully Bill just went to work every day so my financial worries had abated slightly and soon the necessity of children's needs became my salvation. My world soon resumed – cooking the meals, cleaning the house and catering for the needs of my five children in this year of 1937. My first task, after our move, was to write to Elsie and Renee, but at this stage life in Belfast was a reminder of a melancholy that hovered over my shoulder like an insidious insect. One evening I took the plunge and took out Renee's letter in an attempt to create a reply.

240 Great Eastern Highway
Rivervale
16th September 1938

My dearest sisters Renee and Elsie

Thank you so much for the money which you gave me so that I could return to Ireland and see you all. Nothing would make me happier than to see you again and I almost weep to think of the great distance that separates us. I miss you so much and often I feel so lonely, but it is important that I do not dwell on that. I have Bill working close by and I have five lovely children who fill up my life.

Yes, I should have had six children and now is the time to tell you of my sad news. I can barely put pen to paper and this is the reason for my delay in writing to you. Our last child, Pauline, died at the age of three. She had Pneumonia and simply faded away one day. I took her to the hospital, but she went into a permanent slumber that night and the only consolation is that I was with her when she stopped breathing. You see, I cannot even say the word 'died'. I cannot speak of events after her passing, but it is suffice to say that she was buried in Karrakatta, where I will join her one day. You can imagine now why I delayed in writing to you.

There is another reason, too, for my delay. I had been thinking that the money you kindly sent for me, and three children to visit you, was like an early Christmas present and that is how I viewed it. Then I faced the dilemma of which three children I should bring with me. I had thought that I would bring the three youngest ones and then put the three oldest into boarding school. There is a Catholic boarding school a short distance away. Honestly Renee and Elsie, the idea of separating the children like that nearly broke my heart. I discussed it with Bill and he thought that was a good idea. Then we lost Pauline. I am sure you can imagine my pain and it did remind me of the time when we lost our mother and the feeling of numbness that just lingered for so long afterwards.

I do not wish to dwell on sadness too much and now I will tell you something to help lift your spirits and it will lift mine too. As you can see by the date it is my thirty-eighth birthday today and I feel my connections to our family. We have bought this house that is close to the centre of Perth and Bill could continue to work with animals on a milk run and a small dairy at the end of a close-by street.

I have a lovely neighbour again, Mrs Casey, who looks after the children in the case of an emergency. That's right, I promised to lift our spirits!! Well, Mr Casey owns a paper shop on our corner and every morning I walk there. Guess what we do there? Wait for it!! We listen to the news on the wireless! It is large and brown, like a box really, with a lot of crackling when we listen – I say we, because all the neighbours crowd into the shop for this daily event. It is amazing. There hasn't been much hot weather yet but as summer approaches and more people crowd into this tiny shop, I can imagine the smell of all that sweat. Honestly, this is such a hot place to live and a lot of sweaty bodies close together will smell very unpleasant.

As I have listened to the news I feel a sense of almost fear and dread for you. Is Hitler as terrifying as he is made out to be? While it all seems so far away for us here, the events seem quite troubling. It also influenced my thinking about returning home to see you all. Just imagine if I could not return to Australia to join the children. I nearly wrote the word "home".

Sometimes I feel so torn but the idea of being separated from the children is something I could never imagine even in my worst nightmare. I regularly check myself and remind myself that home is Australia. There, I've said it!

Of course, just about everyone here is from some country in Europe. We even had some Chinese people living close by in Safety Bay and when Bill was away on the farm, he saw quite a few Aborigines. He said they mainly stick to themselves, but I guess, they are like us and believe that family is important. There are Italian people who speak in their own language and find it difficult to ask for things in the shop but pointing always seems to work. Just imagine how hard it would be if we didn't speak English! No-one seems to be better off or worse off than anyone else. All the kids seem to just get on with the business of surviving from day to day.

All the children are at school each day and even little Beulah has just started this year. I walk with them every morning to the nearby school, just up the hill and in the afternoon, if it is hot, I take them for a swim in the river, which is close by. Locals call it The Springs and at this stage I haven't quite worked out why.

My dearest sisters, I do hope all is well and I am pleased to end this letter on a happy note after such a sad beginning. I will endeavour to write more frequently now that I have imparted my sadness to you.

I remain your loving sister forever

Flo.

Chapter Nineteen

The War Begins

I returned home on the day, soon after my birthday in 1939, after listening to the radio in the paper shop, absolutely shocked, though I shouldn't have been. International tensions had been building up for some time and this was why I couldn't return to Ireland and leave my children behind. Germany had just invaded Poland and I was worried that Australia would align itself with Britain against Germany. Soon after that our Australian Prime Minister announced that Australia was at war too. The general talk was that it wouldn't last long and hopefully it would be over by Christmas. The talk also consisted of someone having to put Hitler in his place and this invasion of Poland would provide the spark needed to mobilise troops to quash the Germans.

My legs felt weak as I started the daily chores and I found it difficult to concentrate on hanging the washing on the wire stretched out between two posts in the back yard. It was windy and stormy that day, perhaps indicating a sign of events to come as the sheets regularly flapped and blew in my face.

"Bill, we are at war!! I don't know what that means for us!" I blurted out as Bill kicked off his boots on the verandah, wiped the sweat from his brow and walked through the door that evening. The children always ran to meet him and tell him the events of their day, so he was hearing words coming from all directions.

"I know what it means. I'll sign up and take up where I left off. Actually, it'll be interesting when I do because the army had me recorded as leaving the force in 1932. Can't they get anything right!? No, I don't suppose they can. With my past experience I should get a decent wage and just enter where I left off. Anyway, I must go to Safety Bay next week, or sometime soon, to finalise our house business and when I do, I'll sign up then. Get the children to make something and I'll give it to Mrs Mason."

Bill was always authoritative and abrupt, but he loved us all and this was important. I remembered back to the day when he had dismissed the priest when we were living in Aberdare Road, thinking at the time how nonchalant he could be. He just didn't care about the finer things in life.

As we sat down for dinner that night my head was in a whirl, with children's voices chattering about this and that. Audrey sat in her usual chair next to the sink so she could drag the chair into position after dinner to wash the dishes. This was her job and she was such a willing helper that I don't know what I would have done without her. She loved little Beulah and the love was reciprocated. Beulah was a social child and her radiant personality reflected onto us all. Wherever she went she made friends easily and Audrey loved that. I could see that Beulah initiated friendships and Audrey would join in and I was happy it was an arrangement that suited both. Heather adored Bill and the two eldest girls developed their own strong personalities which they needed to survive.

As the eldest, Kathleen was in charge and Moreen regularly challenged her but not as often as Kathleen challenged me. Often, I gave in to her as it was the easiest option and in hindsight I can see that it didn't really matter. With Pauline's death, Kathleen proved that she was a capable leader of the family and this was a relief for me. I wasn't quite sure where these leadership skills came from but in time I would discover that she was a lot like her father. Her strength later provided strength for me, and for that I would be eternally grateful, and in awe.

Summer set in early that year and, as I was doing the washing one day, the children raced home from school and burst through the door.

"Mummy, you are covered in sweat and I can see it running down your face!" shouted Moreen as she was leading the pack. But it was Kathleen who had more important information to impart. I wiped my hands on my apron and looked at the children who had sweat running off their faces too.

"Is it true there is going to be a war?" asked Kathleen.

Luckily it marked Bill's entry – he'd been standing there at the back.

"Well, there will be a war but it will be over by Christmas and I'll be home early in the new year. I'll be leaving from Albany next week and the bus will leave Perth just after the weekend. You can come into town and wave me off. How does that sound?"

"Daddy, we would love that. It means we will ride on a bus and miss school for the day." Heather's comment was agreed by all.

Cairo.

Dearest Flo

I have had leave to come into Cairo to fix up some things that I wanted to get fixed and now I have time to send you a note to let you know how I am going. I will post this letter later today. Look, some bloke even lent me a horse! I hope you show the photo to the girls.

We had a good trip from Albany though the seas were rough at times. Some of the blokes were sea-sick but thankfully they stayed at the end of the boat away from us all. The food has been pretty ordinary, and no-one can serve up a meal as good as you, Flo. I hope those kids appreciate what a good cook you are. You are also a very good mother.

We are based here in North Africa preparing to have a run-in with the Jerries and some of the fellows are getting a bit impatient for some action to put Hitler in his place. It is nearly Christmas and they were told it would be over by Christmas and they are disappointed that they must simply practise their shooting all day. When they aren't engaged in drills then they are working out their cricket team to see who can beat who. They want me to be their captain, so I probably will.

I have been looking for someone that I know but at this stage I haven't seen anyone. Lots of the others know each other as recruitment was centred on each town one at a time. That's why I am surprised that I am captain of the cricket team. It is pretty quiet here but if word comes through then we could well be on the move and then the boys can put their skills into action. I can feel the tension building and I don't think it's all about the cricket. It is shaping up to be very similar to last time when those Germans got too big for their boots.

I don't know when I can write again. It will probably be just as we are about to come home after putting some Jerries in their place. Make sure the kids don't play up.

Your loving husband, Bill

I received Bill's letter on Kathleen's fourteenth birthday in March, and I thought this was a good omen. As I wasn't a spiritual person it didn't do any good to pray or give thanks, but our Kathleen was always one for cheering us all up with her liveliness. For this I was grateful, and I loved the strength I saw in my first born.

Only on birthdays did I think of my two departed babies, but with each passing year the pain grew less. Kathleen's birthday fell on a Friday that year so, when the children came home from school, their treat would be a swim in the Swan River. We walked along the dirt track heading north along the Great Eastern Highway until we came to the street for the river, then a short walk through scrub until an opening where green bull rushes grew. It marked the entry of a natural spring which ran into the river. The locals had named the area 'The Springs'.

I was always mindful of snakes as the weather was warm and humid, a typical day in March. It was late afternoon when we arrived so there were many people swimming already as the children prepared to swim and I prepared to spread my towel out, enjoy the warmth and watch them. Sometimes there were people I knew there and in recent times the number of men had dwindled due to the war. I was grateful at these times for the years we had spent in Safety Bay where all the children had overcome their fear of water and had learnt to swim

Some time had passed, and I was beginning to think of dinner when I heard some loud screaming which raised me from my inertia. I'd had my eyes shut but I quickly raised myself from a towel to see what all the commotion was about. As I walked towards the river I was in time to see some older boys pull a youngster from the water and lay him on the sand face upwards. It didn't take me long to realise he had drowned, and his spirit was no longer with us.

I moved towards the child and soon Kathleen was there to take charge. Very quietly she put a towel over his whole body ensuring that his face was covered, and she closed his eyes with her hands. Soon other adults hovered around, and this was my cue to take my brood home, give them some dinner and hope the sight of dead person hadn't had too much of an impact on them.

Florence and Kathleen in 1950.

Chapter Twenty

The Ending of the War

Of course, the war didn't finish at Christmas, not the first one or the second one, and Bill was away for many years. I became close friends with my neighbours from the corner paper shop and soon Mrs Casey had taken the place of my Safety Bay pseudo-mother, Mrs Mason. I continued to make pies to sell but my financial struggle decreased as the war cheques were deposited into my bank account each month. I felt embarrassed that I'd had to use my Ireland fare from years ago as a means of subsistence and I promised my Irish family that one day I would return to see them all.

I wrote to them from time to time, but I knew that my "Irishness" was diminishing and my "Australianness" was increasing, but this didn't concern me too much as I was surrounded by migrants in this new country and we all had our idiosyncrasies. There were some days when I marvelled at how we all communicated with each other in this land that was still quite strange.

Then one day I received a letter from Bill.

"Why are you so surprised?" asked Mr Casey as he handed me the mail.

I wasn't quite sure what my answer was, but I probably mumbled some inaudible response. I was in shock because I had ceased thinking about him long ago and had been waiting for a letter to inform me that he had been killed in action. This was the first letter

I had received from him for years and my hand shook as I looked at the familiar handwriting. I had been waiting to see this handwriting for so long that it was enough to make my heart pound with fear and uncertainty.

"I think you'd better sit down," said Mrs Casey as she handed me a glass of water.

I could feel the blood drain from my face as she went to the door and put up the sign to indicate the shop was closed. I couldn't stop my eyes from tearing up as all the emotion and hardship I'd felt just spilled over as I opened the envelope with great trepidation. I sat there crying until I had the courage to start reading, with Mrs Casey's hand on my shoulder.

Inverness Scotland 1946

Dearest Flo

Many years have passed, and I have not been able to write to you and for that I am truly sorry. I thought we'd give the Jerries a bit of a hiding but in truth they gave us one. Our troops were in Greece as we were put into groups – I was in the 2nd Eleventh battalion as a Regimental Sergeant Major Warrant Officer 1 or 2. I can't seem to remember now and of course it doesn't matter. In effect, I was the one barking out the orders in front. I guess you think I could be good at that!!! Well, it didn't all go to plan and when we were in Crete we were captured by the Jerries and trucked up through Greece and into a place in Germany near Frankfurt. Bloody Jerries kept us there until the war finished and that is why I couldn't write to you. Did you think I was alive? Remember I told you that I would be safe! Although I was safe they gave us a real hiding.

The place was officially named Stammlager X111C or the nickname was Stalag 13. Stalag means prisoner of war in German and this place in Hammelburg is where I spent many years. There were POWs arriving by train all the time from all over Europe, even Russia. About twenty of us from our battalion were captured and by the time that happened I knew all the blokes. We were all good mates. Do you remember that in my last letter they wanted to make me captain of the cricket team when we were in Egypt? Well, they wanted me to continue being captain, so captain, I was! Right up until the time the Yanks drove their big tanks through their front gate. It was very difficult being captain and keeping the men's spirits up when blokes were dying all around us. Eventually many gave up and some I reckon even died of a broken spirit, but most died through starvation and disease.

I got sick of seeing that swastika everywhere and when the war was coming to an end, the Jerries were running out of food. Many fellows were sick and malnourished, with morale at an all-time low. Serbian food packages kept us all alive so that was our saviour. I tried to be their captain, and that was a great honour for me. It really kept me going as I knew I had to be strong for others. I guess I am surprised that I survived but I did promise you that. Remember? I just couldn't come home by Christmas. Bloody Jerries! Anyway, I should be home by this Christmas and I look forward to seeing you and our girls. Guess they have all grown up now.

I am currently staying with Meg – in the Head Teacher's House in Inverness. Remember that – 71 Kings Street? What a climb up too. Well, that hill is still as steep and is a bit of a battle to climb. She's still pretty bossy so with two bosses in the house I don't know how long I'll be here for. I will be home as soon as I can.

Your loving husband

Bill

My emotions were all over the place as I placed my letter in the envelope and returned home to tell the children their father was alive. They were rather ambivalent about the whole matter and I realised they were so young when he left. True to his word, Bill did come home for Christmas and it should have been a joyous occasion and I had such high hopes for a great reunion.

It was rather a strain for us all and I realised the children had made a cosy nest with their mother and I wasn't sure how their father was going to settle in. Kathleen and Moreen were such good organisers and I had my doubt about how a Warrant Officer from the services was going to recreate himself into Bill Brown civilian again.

Later Bill was awarded a Member of the British Empire for the work he did in the POW camp and was commemorated for his distinguished war efforts.

Some months passed, and our life resumed a normality so that Bill's homecoming blended into something that would happen in the future. The children continued with school each day and after school they would walk with others in the neighbour towards Perth and play around the cement works which constantly poured out soot from its funnel into the air which often blew our way in the afternoon sea breeze. The bridge near the river was a playground for the children as they took turns in jumping into the river. It was quite a dangerous pursuit with the older boys often taking risks and showing off in front of their friends. They came home each night ready for dinner and the telling of the day's events took place around the kitchen table.

They were counting the days until their father came home, an event the whole neighbourhood looked forward to, and the children were very excited. We were expecting him home around our birthdays – Bill's was in October; mine was in September

He arrived home mid-afternoon one day and I had been gardening in the front yard. I heard the gate click and looked up to see a man on our front path. I was surprised and soon I assumed a formal politeness as we exchanged niceties about the weather.

Arriving home during the day gave me a chance to see him as the man who left more than six years ago. But he wasn't that man; the Bill who occupied space in our home was a stranger I had to get used to all over again. His features were sharper, and he looked much older that his 47 years. In many ways he reminded me of my father, not the young energetic man who'd been with us when we first moved into the Rivervale house. His uniform looked too big on him and he went to great lengths to tell me he was still in the forces. He showed me his medals from the war, but it meant very little to me and I could see the persona that had enveloped him in his years away had become his new identity.

I wasn't sure how the children would react and when they arrived home from school, shyness reigned. I could see they were anxious to leave the room. In turn, each child had to shake his hand and say, "Hello Daddy." This was something Bill insisted on and a new tone of formality had just entered the room.

At dinner that night he tried to ask them about school, but they quickly ate their dinner and escaped to the back garden as soon as they could. I tried to fill in the gaps during the silences of the conversations, but I found this a strain.

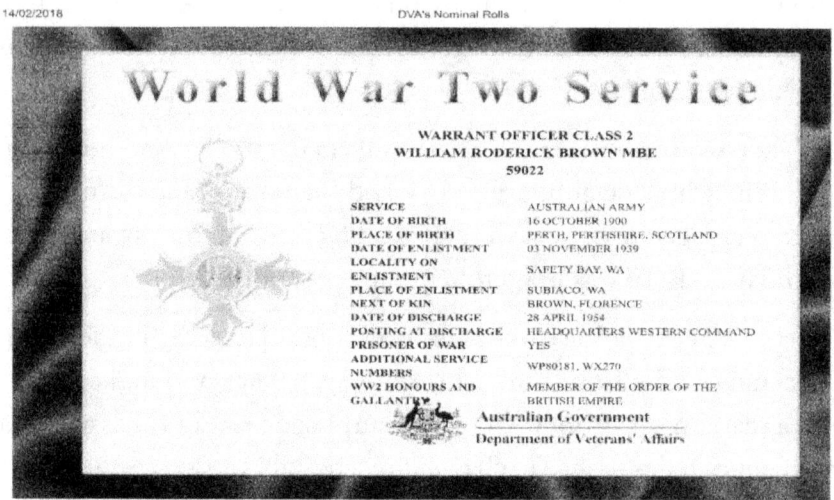

Audrey always washed the dishes after each meal so I suggested to Bill that we go into the lounge and play cards. This proved a good way of filling in time. I guess I was not surprised to feel the tension of a newcomer in the house, but it seemed to pervade into all the spare spaces in the house. I told myself it would get better in time.

As the weeks went past I realised that only when he went to work at Irwin Barracks could I relax. My first cigarette for the day was often straight after he left and I could think about the tasks for the day. My walk to the paper shop on the corner to listen to the daily broadcasts continued and Mrs Casey comforted me by encouraging me to give Bill time to relax and get to know his family again.

I continued making pies to sell at the shop; I cooked Bill's favourite meals and I tried hard to be a good wife in all the ways that mattered. I knew that time would make life a bit easier, but I took on a worried look and a feeling of great anxiety that went with it. Even Mrs Casey stopped asking about our life and instead began talking constantly about the weather.

Ultimately, my emotions took another downward spiral as Bill started organising his family in much the same way as he had organised his troops in the POW camp. I couldn't iron his shirts right and the children had to line up for dinner.

With Kathleen approaching twenty and the other girls almost young women, life became a constant battle. As for Bill, this was one battle he couldn't control. He didn't like Moreen's dancing partner, Jimmy, sleeping on the back verandah from time to time and he became a dark and difficult presence in the house for the girls and their friends. The raised voices and the children's timid behaviour was something new in our household. Soon Bill left and lived elsewhere, and our family became another victim in the aftermath of war.

It took me a long time to recover from the emotional ordeal and I felt guilty for the relief I felt with his sudden but amicable departure. We were two different people now, and trying to fit into a mould that had changed shape over a course of many years was a struggle at best. Needless to say, the eldest girls were the organisers and the younger children, particularly Audrey, were the workers. It was an arrangement which worked well. I was sure each person felt relief when our old routine returned but nothing was said. Soon anxiety became melancholy and then it became peace.

I didn't really miss Bill any more than I missed my Belfast family. They were people who had come in and out of my life and here I was in Australia with a growing family of beautiful girls.

Now I had a future to look forward to and with each passing year I grew stronger. Bill's army wages continued to be deposited into my bank account as he remained in the services for years to come. This sustained us and soon my children would grow up with lives of their own.

When Bill died I continued to receive the war widow's pension and my children and their children became my sustenance. I loved seeing them come to visit but I also loved seeing them go as this allowed me to slip into my reverie in the same lounge chair each night with my bag of sweeties in one hand and a packet of cigarettes in the other, and think of my life in Belfast and in Australia. I was lonely at times but content with the rough road of my existence.

Beulah with the author, Lyn Bodycoat, in 2017.

ABOUT THE AUTHOR

Lyn Bodycoat is a retired English teacher who lives in Perth. She has taught English overseas, in the country and more recently, in various high schools in Perth. She is currently employed as an educational supervisor for three of Perth's universities. Lyn also enjoys spending time with family and friends, as well as travelling.

www.ingramcontent.com/pod-product-compliance
Lightning Source LLC
Chambersburg PA
CBHW070953080526
44587CB00015B/2296